THE BUTTERFLY SECRET

MY JOURNEY FROM RELIGION TO REVOLUTION

BISHOP WAYNE MALCOLM

www.fast-print.net/store.php

The Butterfly Secret

www.wayne@icanministries.co.uk

ISBN: 978-178035-594-8

Cover design & layout by David Springer

First published 2012 by
FASTPRINT PUBLISHING
Peterborough, England.

An environmentally friendly book printed and bound in England by
www.printondemand-worldwide.com

This book is made entirely of chain-of-custody materials

Dedication

This book is dedicated to the New Breed of ambitious, anointed and amphibious believers who sense a call to social significance and who dream of making a difference in the world. Those who are engaged in the struggle for social justice, for economic opportunity and for the end of poverty! You are not afraid of the dark houses because you are the light of the world. You are not afraid of corrupt institutions because you are the salt of the earth. Your ambitions are uncommon but you have grace for your space. You are anointed to change the world from the inside out.

Although you faithfully commit time, talent and treasure to your church; you don't want to be a flashlight in the daylight. Instead your uncommon ambition is to impact industries and institutions with your gifts and skills. You are not enamoured with a role in the church as much as you are with a role in the world.

The blessing of Joseph is on you as is the beauty of Esther. The determination of Nehemiah is in you as is the courage of Daniel. You are called to serve God in the Kingdoms of men but are frequently misunderstood, mis-represented and mis-quoted by your religious brothers and sisters. May this book explain the mystery of your own path and give you the peace of knowing that God is in control!

ACKNOWLEDGMENTS

I wish to acknowledge the many people who have loved, supported, helped and covered me during the years of transformation. Your contributions to my life have been noted in both heaven and earth. Without you this story would read differently and its conclusions may not have been so hopeful. You have all enriched my experience and filled my thoughts with precious memories.

I firstly want to acknowledge my amazing mother. She is a tower of faith and strength with wisdom and discretion from beyond this world. Thank you for the solace, the comfort and the friendship that we have. Many in your generation don't understand how a mother and son can sit together and laugh the way that we do. Little did I know that my transformation was an answer to your prayers. Every time that I shed my skin, it is as though you knew what was happening and celebrated the change. My love for you goes beyond these words: You are simply the best mother in the world.

My boys Reuben and Andrew are the most amazing gifts from God. Not only have I loved to watch them grow but I love the fact that we are all young men. We enjoy each other's company and can reason like friends. Only we know how thick and deep is the bond of love between us and only God knows what we endured together. You are the children of prophecy and destiny and the crown of the anointing is upon you both. You will be, do and have more than I have imagined and raise the bar for generations to come. You are simply the best of the best and my prayers are with you.

Reverend Dr Tim McClure, you are one in a zillion. You became my mentor and model when I was 17 years old. I wanted to preach like you, dress like you and change peoples lives like you. You saw something in me that I couldn't see in myself and took me under your wing as a boy preacher to nurture my destiny. I'm not sure that anyone understood the depth of our friendship or the length of it. For almost 30 years we have run up each others phone bills, travelled together, dreamed together, cried together and preached together. Most of all we have laughed a whole lot. You were there for me at every major turn in my life and although you are not named in this book, you are there on every page. Thank you dear friend. The next 30 years will be awesome!

Pastor David Springer, God chose you to be the pastor of our church because you are the most loving, kind, non-judgemental, supportive and caring individual I know. You stuck with me even when I was trying to leave myself. You are like Shem and Japheth who covered their father and preserved his dignity. When I was going through the worst, you simply stayed faithful to God and stayed committed to me. May God give you more than you can store and continue to bless your life with manifold favour.

What can I say of the many ministers who knowingly or unknowingly helped me to make and to survive the transition. The list is endless but I would like to pay special tribute to Bishop's Tudor Bismarck, T D Jakes, Noel Jones, Wayne Pugh, Dr Mark Hanby, Richard Heard, John Francis and the late Norman L Wagner. In your own way you each touched my life and showed me another side of Jesus.

To my church family, particularly those who endured the cocoon years and held me up in prayer, I say a big thank you. When my hands were tired, you lifted them up so we could all win the battle. And to the new comers who have met me on the other side; you inspire me and your authenticity makes me proud to be your Bishop.

To my many personal friends, I want to thank you all for allowing me to be me. In particular I am grateful for the friendship of Pastor Errol Graham who has the gift of faith and never fails to boost mine when its weak. To Matt Bird who introduced me to the art of unwinding and to a growing world of white friends. To Patricia Burrowes, who started out as a secretary but has since worn any hat necessary to advance the ministry. To Marlow Morris who watched over me and my boys like a guardian angel for over a decade of unbroken commitment. Your contributions to my life have made a profound difference.

Finally, I want to acknowledge the amazing grace of a good God to whom I give all the honour and the glory for my story!

TABLE OF CONTENTS:

THE BUTTERFLY

A man found a cocoon of a butterfly. One day a small opening appeared. He sat and watched the butterfly for several hours as it struggled to force its body through that little hole. Then it seemed to stop making any progress. It appeared as if it had gotten as far as it could, and it could go no further.

So the man decided to help the butterfly. He took a pair of scissors and snipped off the remaining bit of the cocoon. The butterfly then emerged easily. But it had a swollen body and small, shrivelled wings.

The man continued to watch the butterfly because he expected that, at any moment, the wings would enlarge and expand to be able to support the body, which would contract in time. Neither happened! In fact, the butterfly spent the rest of its life crawling around with a swollen body and shrivelled wings. It never was able to fly.

What the man, in his kindness and haste, did not understand was that the restricting cocoon and the struggle required for the butterfly to get through the tiny opening were God's way of forcing fluid from the body of the butterfly into its wings so that it would be ready for flight once it achieved its freedom from the cocoon.

Sometimes struggles are exactly what we need in our lives. If God allowed us to go through our lives without any obstacles, it would cripple us. We would not be as strong as what we could have been. We could never fly!

Author unknown.

INTRODUCTION

This introduction was written after most of the other chapters in this book were completed. Had I started with it, the book may have taken another direction. Instead, I wanted it to grow organically out of my memories and recollections of the events that would eventually shape my life and work. Starting at the end is not a bad idea because it informs the way that you organise the information. It also ensures that you stay on track and eventually reach your goal.

This book is NOT an autobiography although it is written in autobiographical style. It omits huge chunks of valuable experiences that likewise contributed to the person I am now. While valuable, these experiences make more sense in a full blown autobiography. What I attempt to do here is to document the theological and philosophical transformation that happened in my head. It is more a glimpse into my mind than it is into my life. Although I make many references to actual experiences, they are only there to aide your comprehension of what was happening inside.

You will also note that I don't mention other people or organisations by name even though the temptation to do this was, at times, great. This is because the book is about my subjective (internal) experience and not my (objective one). It is about me and the events that contributed to my philosophical transformation. I attempt to keep you inside my mind as we journey from chapter to chapter.

It has also been chronologically difficult to arrange. Real life is multi-faceted so that many things are happening at the same time. When writing, you pretty much have to list one thing at a time which may give the illusion that one thing happens after the other. Life is complex and difficult to capture in writing. I really do applaud those authors who can successfully paint pictures with their pens in such a way that the reader is transported back through time to relive the emotion of the moment. Unfortunately I am still working on that and as it is my first attempt at writing from this perspective I ask that you bear with me if it comes across as lecturing.

What follows is a frank and often brutal exposé of those defining moments that moved me from legalism to grace, from depression to deliverance and from church to the Kingdom. Anyone meeting me today, who knew me 20 years ago would quickly conclude that this guy has changed. Yes I have and this book explains both how and why. I wish I could say that all these changes occurred through inspiration and passion however that would be far from true. Many of the changes were the results of desperation and pressure. Much of my life was moulded in dark places of solitude and emotional pain.

I likewise didn't give a title to this work until it was nearly finished. I looked for a metaphor that would explain and summarise my story of transformation and I found it in the butterfly. Born a caterpillar and constantly shedding its skin until it finally spins a cocoon and endures a season of darkness and solitude. Its transformation occurs in the darkness and solitude of a painful and difficult place. But it emerges from the cocoon with wings, colour, grace and power to become the butterfly that everybody loves.

I realised that if the butterfly could be interviewed and asked on national TV what the secret of its beauty and brilliance was, it would say; "I wasn't born this way, but I became this way through the numerous sheddings of my skin and through the painful process of transformation which occurred in my darkest hours." That was it. I had found the metaphor for my story; hence I call it the butterfly secret.

My goal is to encourage those who now find themselves on the pathways of purpose, courageously following their convictions but discouraged by the darkness that following your convictions brings. Following your convictions is a choice. You can choose to ignore them in an attempt to sustain the security that comes with stagnation, or you can boldly go where you have never gone before, trusting that God will never lead you where his grace cannot keep you.

Many leaders operate like masked super heroes in which the real man or woman is (disguised/concealed/shrouded) by a myth. Removing the mask and exposing the man is difficult but necessary if the next generation is to go, grow and glow beyond the limits set by this one. While perpetuating the myth may produce more popularity; empowering the man will produce more power. As for this butterfly; it was once a caterpillar and my wings grew when my religion collapsed. In the darkness of depression and personal failure, my capacity to fly was created. Hopefully someone reading my story will relate to a principle or a pattern that releases them to become the butterfly they were born to be.

CHAPTER 1

CONVERSION

My Christian journey started out in Poplar, East London. I was only 15 years old at the time and was making the most of the annual 6 week school holidays. At that age, hanging out with friends and devising mischief was my favourite pass-time. –°°However, on this day of mid-august 1982, my life would change. Out of the blue, a young lady approached a group of us and invited us to a church service that was already in progress. It was just around the corner and we had nothing to lose. Obviously, I had my eye on the girl and had no fear of a church service, so I went without hesitation. Upon arrival, I quickly lost interest in the girl because the Pentecostal service itself now had my full attention. So I didn't get the girl but what I did get, started me on a journey for which I am eternally grateful. It's a journey of adventure, with high risks and equally high rewards. It's taken me round the world, put me on TV, given me an audience in Parliament and introduced me to the most amazing people. Not even I could have guessed that I would become a Bishop and Christian leader in the years to come. But that's exactly what happened!

I was quite advanced at 15, looking older than my age and hanging out with friends who were 2 and 3 years older than I was. In my head, I was a Rastafarian, but in appearance I looked like any ordinary teenaged black boy. I loved the Rastafarian movement and seized every opportunity to go to the clubs and venues where roots reggae music was played.

Rastafarianism anchored my faith in God and seeded in me a desire for freedom and social justice. Of course the music was hot too.

It offered me a cultural education and seemed to explain the injustice of racism that was so blatant in the late 70's and early 80's. It was an anti-colonial movement that sought to liberate; first the mind and then the body from all forms of colonial oppression. Rastafarianism anchored my faith in God and seeded in me a desire for freedom and social justice. Of course the music was hot too. I still love it and still have the utmost respect for the true followers of the religion and for anyone who engages in the struggle for social justice.

I think this is why it was easy for me to accept Christ as Saviour. I was already quite spiritual and read the Bible often but God was still a transcendent mystery to me. On that visit to church though, I experienced something unique. My pre-conceived notions of Christianity were completely shattered. It looked like God was literally with these people and young people at that! They worshipped from the heart, they shouted hallelujah, they spoke in tongues, they preached with passion. It was as though God was real to them and all I knew, was that I wanted him to be that real to me. So I responded to an altar call, gave my heart to Christ, got baptised and shortly after experienced the baptism of the Spirit. Now I was one of them; speaking in tongues, all night prayer, studying the Scriptures, witnessing for the Lord and all the rest.

CONVERSION

Wayne had changed and it shocked everyone. You see, I was the least likely person to become a Christian. I loved my reggae music and marijuana spliffs way to much to give it all up for Christ. But give it up I did to become a tongue-talking Pentecostal. Of course I dived in. I had no choice. Everyone around me wanted to know what, why, how, where and when? I needed answers. My friends had a plethora of arguments against Christianity and tried everything to get me back the way I used to be. My answer to most of their questions in the beginning was this: "I don't know the answer to that one but I'll find out!" I started studying and studying and studying so I could answer questions about my faith. It was important to me that Christianity made rational sense and that its claims could be justified. The end result was that I became a great debater who knew how to answer difficult questions about Christianity.

Please remember I've now turned 16 and although most of my time was spent praying, studying, witnessing and attending church, I was still growing up and had to deal with those dreaded hormones. The church had lots of rules around the idea of freedom from sin and separation from the world. We dare not break the church rules because this would be a sin against God and secondly because the church would punish those who broke the rules. Punishment could mean anything from being sent to Coventry (no one will talk to you); to being silenced (come to church, sit at the back and say nothing); to excommunication from the church altogether.

The most difficult of all the church rules was the rule of celibacy until marriage. The church back then was quite strict. You couldn't date or express an interest in the opposite sex unless you had intentions of marriage. To cap it all; chastity and pre-marital celibacy were preached so hard that most of us believed we would miss the rapture and go to hell if we failed in this area. I'm sure our preachers meant well, but the extreme emphasis on this subject generated a warped view of marriage. Most of us got married in our early 20's for one solitary reason: it was better to marry than to burn (in hell). So I did get married at age 20. After all I was going into the ministry and couldn't allow the enemy an opportunity to bring me down. From that marriage, two wonderful children: who I'll talk about later in the book.

OLD SCHOOL

Needless to say, I started my journey in a traditional setting. Women wore hats and long skirts. Men wore suits and ties. Total separation from the world was a must. The clubs went, the music went, the friends went and so did any form of worldly entertainment. It all had to go. Although everyone meant well and was sincere in their attempts to please God, the underlying ethos was legalism. Legalism is a theological term used to sum up the belief that salvation is only possible for those who obey the Old Testament laws or who keep the church's rules. So we were saved, only if we kept the rules. If we broke them we were not saved and would probably miss the rapture (second coming of Christ for his church). I didn't mind the legalism; In fact, I loved it because it provided the perfect cage for my lion. It protected me from the world; it kept me celibate until marriage and prevented me from sliding back into the old paths. The stricter, the better because under that regime there was simply no way back.

The problem with legalism is that it can only ever cage the lion but can never tame it. Because it is based on a false interpretation of the gospel, it generates a warped view of Christ. In legalism, Christ is depicted as a cold judge who is going to send people to hell for simply misunderstanding Scripture let alone disobeying it. This meant it wasn't just the world in danger of hell fire; it was all of us too. We could all go to hell if we missed one point.

THE MAIN POINT

Although hell was reserved for those who disobeyed the teaching of Scripture, there was one main point that concerned the group I was with. The group is known by many names including Jesus only, Oneness Pentecostals and the Apostolic faith. The main point of contention was the wording used at your baptism. We firmly believed that water baptism by full immersion was a necessary part of being saved. In other words, you weren't saved without it. We went one step further and insisted that your baptiser used the Jesus only formula and not the Trinitarian one. In other words, the baptiser had to say: 'I now baptise you in the name of Jesus Christ'. as opposed to 'I now baptise you in the name of the Father and of the Son and of the Holy Spirit'. We taught that the 'Name' of the Father, the Son and the Spirit was in fact: Jesus Christ because Jesus embodied all that God is.

We cited the fact that early Christian baptisms used the Jesus only formula and that the Triune formula was only mentioned once in Scripture and that it was clearly misinterpreted by the Trinitarians. The problem was that we made it a 'salvation issue'. Absolutely no one was saved without a correct water baptism. Of course there were other attachments including speaking with tongues, rejecting the Trinitarian version of God and practising obedience to Christian teaching, but the main one was the baptism.

These ideas had a huge effect on my development as a minister and later as a pastor. You see the first 10 years of my Christian experience was informed by this theology. I embraced it, believed it, preached it with passion and tears and defended it to the last in numerous debates and discussions. I was a oneness, apostolic, Jesus name Pentecostal. No shame in my game; it was my way or the highway. In fact, I took it to such an extreme level that I became known as a champion of the message and a defender of the faith.

When I finally started a church at the ripe age of 21; it was founded on this doctrine and within a few years I was the leader of one of Britain's fastest growing churches. I mean, we went from 5 to 50 in the first year and from 50 to 200 a few years later and from 200 to 1200 over the next seven years. How amazing was that? leading 1200 people in my early 30's with satellite branches and a network of leaders from India to South Africa, from the Caribbean and the Americas. I had arrived at the pinnacle of mount achievement and everyone had their eye on Bishop elect Wayne Malcolm.

I mean, we went from 5 to 50 in the first year and from 50 to 200 a few years later and from 200 to 1200 over the next seven years. How amazing was that?

DOUBTS

By this time we had acquired a disused warehouse with over 40,000 sq ft of derelict rooms and had renovated it into a 1000 seat auditorium, complete with ancillary rooms and office space galore. Regular attendance was in the 900's with standing room only during special services and conferences. My international ministry had taken off and I was literally the darling of the Apostolic faith movement. A young man, with a thriving church, making the headlines and yet fully embracing the Jesus only doctrine, was the pride and joy of my elders, Bishops and overseers.

However I had begun to entertain doubts. I loved all my brethren in the movement and still do, but I started to think the unthinkable. It all started when I began speaking for the Trinitarians. You see, up until that point we had no fellowship with any group that didn't see things our way. But I had become so popular that folks wanted to know me and would invite me to speak at their events. I did it because I thought this would provide a good introduction to our faith. However it allowed me to see and hear things that I otherwise wouldn't have known.

I met real Christians that loved God and loved others, sincerely living out their own revelation of Christ. They were the most kind, caring, considerate and decent people I had met. They were on fire for God and were filled with the same Holy Spirit as me. They exercised spiritual gifts and manifested the fruit of the Spirit. I could see Jesus all over them and it confused me completely. How could these people be lost? Are they really going to hell? It was very confusing because I needed a rational answer. I struggled and grappled with these issues for years before doing or saying anything, even to my closest friends. You see all of my success had been built on a doctrine that I now doubted. It would surely cost me everything to express any doubt at all, let alone to move in another direction. I was stuck and needed answers.

INDIA

In 1997, I went on a mission trip to India. This would be a life changing trip for many reasons. The year before, I was recording a TV show in Israel. On that trip, a friend introduced me to an Indian couple who were on vacation. They were both up in years and had lived a fascinating life. The reason for the introduction was that the lady was determined to get baptised in the river Jordan and she specifically wanted a Pentecostal minister to do it. Of course I agreed and off we went to the river Jordan. The baptism was beautiful and in many ways fulfilled one of my own aspirations, namely; to baptise in the river Jordan. On the way back, she shared with me how that her son was also a minister in India and that he was just like me. When I asked what she meant by that, she just said, "He prays for people and they fall down." I laughed and thought; yep he's Pentecost! Of course I had no idea which side of the baptismal fence he was on, but I guest with some certainty that we both embraced the baptism of the Holy Spirit experience.

Not many months later I received an invitation from her son to conduct a gospel crusade in India and the following year, myself and a team of 15 others were on the plane to Calcutta. Of course the meetings were amazing and the details would require another book. What was most relevant to my theological journey was the way I felt when I finally sat down to discuss Christian doctrine with my new friend. He loved our ministry and I loved his. I was so moved by his devotion and sacrifice for Christ and yet in the back of my mind he was possibly not even saved. My theology at that stage said; unless he is baptised our way; he is not saved. This was difficult to process because his Christianity impressed me. When we did have the discussion about baptism, he explained to me that he believed just like me.

For six months it felt as though I was suspended between time and eternity and as though each moment was my last..

This should have elated me no end but instead it had the opposite effect. I felt deeply ashamed for the fact that I had judged him the whole time. I had pre-judged my brother and had got it all wrong. This experience shook me to the core because for the whole two weeks, I was trying to explain to myself how it was that a Trinitarian could have so much love for Christ and so much power with God. Even though it turns out he shared my beliefs on a number of issues; the experience forced me to negotiate a tension between my beliefs and my experience for two whole weeks. It further opened my mind to a new possibility; namely the possibility that doctrinal differences didn't matter to God.

SICKNESS

Shortly after my return from India, I collapsed in my pulpit from a mystery illness that would last for at least six months. The symptoms were similar to a stroke, however they only came on if I stood up or sat up. If I laid down, I would feel absolutely normal until getting up and then it was like a stroke all over again. The symptoms were obvious but it took a doctor in the US to diagnose the condition. It was rare and incurable but manageable with a concoction of medications. The worse symptoms were psychological, namely; the constant feeling that death was imminent.

For six months it felt as though I was suspended between time and eternity and as though each moment was my last. In that state; peace with God is paramount while your priorities get reconfigured. My sense of what was important changed dramatically and any sense of judgement I had for anyone began to dissipate.

With the help of medication I was able to get to a few church services and conferences. At one such conference I was shocked to find that the guest speaker was a known heretic. By that, I mean someone who used to be just like us but had now left the old doctrines and was operating on the other side of the doctrinal divide. His wife wore makeup and jewellery. She was also known to wear trousers in public. All of these were completely unacceptable to old school Pentecostals. I had heard all sorts about this gentleman and wondered for a minute if the host of the conference had any idea.

Although I was confused by his appearance on the bill, something in me wanted to hear him speak. I remembered the shame I felt in India when I had prejudged my brother and decided that I would lay all judgement aside and forget anything I ever heard about this man. I would just listen with eyes closed and simply feel after God.

Within forty five minutes, this man of God told my life story and made sense of all the non-sense going on in my head. He exposed the error of my ways and opened my eyes to a fresh interpretation of God. It felt as though I had been born again as the spirit of elitism and legalism began to melt away. Again the feeling of shame came with it when I realised how wrong I was about this man. I had judged him based on rumour and criticism coming from religious tyrants who wanted to stigmatise a good man for growing up.

ADVICE

I was beginning to see a marvellous light but had no one to talk to about the implications of what was happening. So I decided to break a fundamental rule: namely to get advice from 'heretics.' You see, there were a few other characters who had successfully made the transition from legalism to grace. But we were warned in no uncertain terms to stay away from them and to have no fellowship with them. I was told all sorts about these characters: they were adulterers, drug dealers and alcoholics. They left the truth and God had turned them over to a reprobate mind. I was to have nothing to do with them. However from my observations they were doing well. They had been embraced by the wider body of Christ and had built successful ministries. Some were pastors but most were itinerate speakers who had large followings and were warmly received.

I decided to contact them and ask for advice. What a shock!! Instead of finding a group of alcoholics, drug dealers and adulterers; I found the most loving, caring and kind individuals who themselves had given up their own pedestals in pursuit of the truth. These individuals were neither elitist nor exclusive. They were humble men who loved God with a passion and wanted his will more than life itself.

This was the beginning of the end and the end of the beginning for me. What I learned was shocking and transformational. In my heart I knew it was the end of the empire

I had built and the beginning of a whole new me. My problem was that I couldn't continue preaching something I no longer believed. Knowing it would cost me everything, I embarked on a journey of study and prayer to determine what I now believed. I needed to know what was important to God and what was not. I wanted to know the truth about salvation, holiness, the second coming and everything else. But I had a dilemma!

THE GREAT DILEMMA.

The dilemma was; do I simply resign and start all over again, or do I attempt to reform the church I had? The advice I got was quiet brutal. I was told that moving a congregation from legalism to grace will take an average of 7 years and that there are no guarantees that anyone will be left.

I really didn't know what to do because I felt responsible for everyone and didn't want to leave anyone behind. I began to count the cost of making the move. I knew I would lose friends, status, much needed finance, members, possibly our facility and may even incur personal losses because the stress may be too much for my family to bear. We had just moved into our own home after living in rented accommodation for years. The boys were in private school and everything was going great. No need to change. Now was not the time to risk everything. Was I being a fool or was God leading me? At times I really didn't know. I just knew that I would study the Scriptures without preconceived notions and arrive at a position that I was ready to live or die for.

CHAPTER 2

ALL CHANGE

It took many years before my deepest theological questions were fully resolved. However I had reached a major conclusion quite early on. Namely that the 'dress code' rules were neither Biblical nor practical. At the time we had a whole set of rules around how people dressed; particularly women, who bore the brunt of our holiness doctrine. They had to have their heads covered in church, they couldn't wear trousers (because that was considered a man's garment) and skirts had to be close to the ankle in length. Nothing revealing at all; no make up or jewellery was permitted at any time and women couldn't cut their hair. Anyone deviating from this script was simply excluded and barred from participating in leadership or ministry.

How oppressive and misogynistic was that? We called it holiness and I preached it with passion and conviction. However, this was the first big test for me because I was determined to bring our church out of the dark ages and modernise it completely, but dropping these rules would have all sorts of ramifications.

Although it took a few years, we eventually changed the look and feel of our church. To my surprise; our ladies actually looked beautiful with different hair styles, different sorts of make up and jewellery, trousers, shapes, figures and even legs. But it all came at a price. I lost most of my religious friends and a good chunk of our membership as they were not sure about this 'new direction'.

Many of those who stayed, still entertained doubts about whether or not this was right or wrong. Remember, they had been raised in legalism and they worshipped an angry God who would send them to hell for even mis-interpreting a passage of Scripture, let alone disobeying it. They were scared but hoped that I knew what I was doing.

A LITTLE LEAVEN

Although we had successfully got passed the archaic and typically Caribbean dress codes so that on the surface we looked quite normal; we were not normal! Allow me to use a Scripture to explain why:

> ***Then Jesus said unto them, Take heed and beware of the leaven of the Pharisees and of the Sadducees... Then understood they how***

that he bade them not beware of the leaven of bread, but of the doctrine of the Pharisees and of the Sadducees.

Matthew 16:6&12

And he charged them, saying, Take heed, beware of the leaven of the Pharisees, and of the leaven of Herod.

Mark 8:15

In the mean time, when there were gathered together an innumerable multitude of people, insomuch that they trode one upon another, he began to say unto his disciples first of all, Beware ye of the leaven of the Pharisees, which is hypocrisy.

Luke 12:1

Jesus here refers to the doctrine of the Pharisees as leaven or yeast. Once yeast is inside a lump of bread, it infects and inflates the entire lump. It becomes indistinguishable from the flour and impossible to separate. These are hard words because it means that a false doctrine can sit in the psyche of an individual or group, affecting everything else; contaminating them on every level and inflating them with pride and arrogance.

This was a problem for me because it was the very doctrine of the Pharisees that we were contaminated with. The doctrine of the Pharisees is legalism.

LEGALISM

Legalism is a theological term used to describe the belief that salvation is only possible for those who keep the law. A legalist is someone who creates conditions for salvation. I.e. keep the Sabbath, get baptised a particular way, don't drink, smoke, go to parties etc. The list is endless of what a legalist will preach against.

Legalism thrives on a threat; specifically the threat of eternal hell fire. A legalistic says; now you believe in Christ, you must do this or that or stop this and stop that or else you will go to hell. As I say, the list is endless of sins that will keep people out of heaven and send them to hell.

A legalistic says; now you believe in Christ, you must do this or that or stop this and stop that or else you will go to hell.

Of course my studies had lead me to a different conclusion. I never entertained the idea that a Christian could do anything or that there were no sins. My doubts were not about sin but about the depth, the length and the heights of grace? I questioned; is there anything my child could do to make me want to put them in the oven on full heat? If your child disobeys you, it may be disappointing, even distressing, but it will never make you want to put them in the oven on full roast! Unless of course, you are a total psychopath. Yet our love for our children pales into insignificance compared with God's love for his.

> ***If ye then, being evil, know how to give good gifts unto your children, how much more shall your Father which is in heaven give good things to them that ask him?***
>
> *Matthew 7:11*

MOSES WENT TO HEAVEN

God's laws (principles) are given for your benefit and not his. Keeping them or breaking them has consequences for you in time but not eternity. Let me show you:

Do you remember why Moses didn't go into the Promised Land? That's right; because he disobeyed God. The judgement was severe, don't you think? After all, he had spent his life in pursuit of this land but through one act of disobedience was not allowed to go in. A legalist would preach this as proof that one act of disobedience is enough to keep you out of heaven; no matter how much good you have done in the past.

However, the Promised Land was not heaven. It was a physical country that was occupied by devil worshippers and cannibals. Hardly a picture of heaven. Moses was not barred from going to heaven because of disobedience; he was barred from making any further progress on planet earth because of his disobedience. Disobedience to Divine principles only ever hinders your progress on earth but has nothing to do with whether or not you go to heaven when you die.

Oh, just in case the legalist still has doubt, please remember that on the Mount of Transfiguration; Jesus was seen with Elijah and guess who?? Moses! The same guy who was barred from the promise land through disobedience, was safe in heaven with Jesus.

MISREADING

Legalism thrives on a misreading of the Old Testament. The problem is that the old covenant between God and Israel was a temporal and earthly covenant. There was no promise of heaven, or threat of hell in it. There were only the blessings of obedience and the curses of disobedience. Each of these blessings and curses had to do with quality of life issues. If you obeyed the law; then long life, health, wealth and happiness would follow. If you disobeyed the law; then death, disease, barrenness and poverty would follow. For the followers of the law; heaven and hell were places on earth. Eternity was a mystery to them and the hereafter was not as important as the here and now.

The mistake I made as a legalist was to assume that obedience to God was a heaven or hell issue rather than a life and death issue. Obedience to Biblical principles will always deliver a better quality of life and disobedience will cause that quality of life to deteriorate. Obedience still brings a blessing and disobedience still brings a curse, but these blessings and curses are all relegated to time and not to eternity as in the case of Moses. Just as obeying or disobeying your parents has consequences but it never changes the way that they love you or the plans they have for you.

A careful reading of the New Testament will show that this issue was the number one challenge facing the early church. There were many who insisted that the Gentiles who came to Christ should be circumcised and keep the law of Moses or they were not saved. This idea caused a big fight in the early church and opened up a huge discussion on the purpose of the law and on the nature of the gospel. The conclusions they reached were clear; Gentiles didn't have to be circumcised neither did they have to keep the law of Moses in order to be saved. You can read about this in Acts 15 and in the entire book of Galatians.

ETERNITY

No person can merit a place in heaven based on their performance. This is the irrefutable teaching of the New Testament. Keep all the rules, all the regs and live an exemplary life of selfless sacrifice and you still don't merit eternal life. The only basis for the Christian hope is the performance of Jesus at the cross. At the cross, Jesus took upon himself the sins of the world and offered his life as full payment for all of our offences. In this respect, sin cannot stop you from going to heaven when you die but it can stop you from enjoying heaven on earth.

I know that this is a difficult idea for those people who were raised in a religion that makes obedience to the rules a prerequisite for heaven. However that difficulty tends to disappear at funerals where a dear saint has left us. We all know that the deceased was not perfect and that they died with flaws that the Bible clearly calls sin. Pride, unbelief, unforgiveness and not doing the good that you know, are all called sins in the Bible. Yet we will sing about heaven and comfort the bereft with sermons about a resurrection, knowing full well that the deceased was not without sin. In fact, if perfect obedience were necessary for heaven, then I can prove that there will only be one person there. Jesus is the only person who emerges from Scripture without spot, wrinkle or blemish. He is the only person who lived a sinless life. Everyone else, including our faith heroes are flawed.

> ***As it is written, There is none righteous, no, not one:***
>
> *Romans 3:10*

> ***For all have sinned, and come short of the glory of God;***
>
> *Romans 3:23*

The Bible, quite deliberately mars the reputations of each of our faith heroes. They were all great in faith but they all came short of the glory of God. This includes the Patriarchs, the prophets and the kings of Israel and Judah. It also includes the Apostles themselves who were no strangers to doubt, fear and shame. The fact that the Bible speaks so openly about the failings and short comings of its own heroes is one of the proofs of its authenticity and inspiration. When men write about themselves they are usually careful to omit anything that they are ashamed of. But if the writing is inspired by God, it will include success and failure, weakness and strength as well as moments of faith and doubt. We know that Noah got shamefully drunk and that David committed murder to cover up his adultery. We also know that Solomon lost the plot and that Elijah became fearful. The list is quite exhaustive but it is there for a reason.

PSYCHOLOGICAL DAMAGE

The main reason why these flaws are recorded in the Bible is to prevent us from creating unhealthy and unattainable expectations from ourselves and others. It is also meant to prevent us from worshipping, idolising and deifying men. People are not perfect in a religious sense; they are only perfect in a human sense. They are perfectly human. Just as a baby that cries, throws up and messes itself is still a perfect baby and is adored by its parents, you too can be a flawed but perfect human being that is loved and cherished by God. Accepting the fact that you are perfectly human and therefore prone to error, should prevent you from creating unrealistic expectations of yourself and of others.

A good reality check coupled with a good Bible search should also protect you from painting a distorted self-portrait. If you see yourself as a worthless failure because you made a mistake, then you will have successfully limited your prospects in life. People who carry a sense of shame, self-disgust and unworthiness through life will never even see, let alone be able to seize the opportunities that God puts before them.

False religious notions do long term psychological damage to people who never feel good enough for God, family, friends and society at large. They are constantly coming up short because their expectations are simply too high. Lets face it; sinless perfection is unrealistic, considering that only one man in history ever achieved it and he was virgin born with Divine blood flowing through his veins. A failure to realise the impossibility of sinless perfection still leads many to cultivate a set of self-defeating beliefs about themselves and about others. The feeling of not being enough and of general unworthiness then creeps into all their relationships with friends and family alike. It destroys their confidence and thereby limits their aspirations. They become their own worse enemy in life because they literally expect to be rejected, turned down, refused and excluded.

BY GRACE, THROUGH FAITH ALONE!

I discovered that we could only ever be saved by grace through faith alone.

> ***For by grace are ye saved through faith; and that not of yourselves: it is the gift of God:***
> ***9] Not of works, lest any man should boast.***
> ***10] For we are his workmanship, created in Christ Jesus unto good works, which God hath before ordained that we should walk in them.***
>
> *Ephesians 2:8-10*

Grace can be defined as unmerited favour. This means that it is unwarranted, undeserved and unconditional. God saves us because He loves us and not because we deserve it. Wow!

The day I realised that God loves me, warts and all, is the day I got delivered from depression and fear. (More about that in the next chapter). I was free and madly in love with Jesus but my church was still infected and inflated by the leaven of the Pharisees in the form of the legalism that I had taught them. My church still struggled with the road to freedom that I was on. Some said I had lost the plot, others said he's backslidden but many simply upped and left. So with a smaller and more volatile crowd, I began the process of teaching grace. The goal was to purge the house of legalism, elitism, exlusivism and pride. I wanted us to become an inclusive crowd that welcomed everyone no matter where they had been or what they had done. I wanted my people to know the grace that I had found.

SOUNDS SOFT

I know that the grace message sounds soft to some people but really the message calls on people to demonstrate extraordinary strength. Here's why: Legalism cages the beast within. It doesn't change a person's nature but only cages it behind rules and regulations. In this respect you will never really see who people are because they are simply not allowed to show it. The moment the rules are gone, and the beast is out of the cage, the real person appears. Grace does not seek to cage your lion but rather to tame it until it can lie down with a lamb.

When I first started teaching grace, I was shocked to see the most pious of women turn up to church with green hair, bright red lipstick, short skirts and noses pierced. When I ask, "What's happened to you sis?" The answer was: "You preached it Bishop, I'm gonna do me..." We would both end up in fits of laughter as I tried to remember the pious sister with her hat, long skirt, sleeves, no figure, no make up and no jewellery.

Of course I knew what was happening: the cage had been opened and the lion was running wild. But it wasn't too long before those same people found themselves and achieved balance. On the other hand, my religious crowd was outraged that I could allow sister so and so to dress like that in church and still have her sing on the choir. They insisted that I do something, say something and stop it now. They even threatened to stop tithing and to leave for a more spiritual church. And leave they did!!

In a legalistic church, people claim to be free from sin, but 'free from sin' is typically a code word which means: scared to sin. No one truly knows if they are free from sin until they are free to sin. If you are free to do it but choose not to then you are free from it. If you are not free to do it then there is no sense singing about freedom from it. Typically a fundamentalist environment acts like the prohibition laws of the 1920's in that it generates an underground movement of sin-secrecy. On the overground it is suppressed, but underground it's alive and kicking.

This is why grace is not soft. It's strong. In fact another definition or application of grace is 'Divine enabling.' Put simply; grace is God's strength compensating for your weaknesses. It is The God given Power to follow a God given path. You see, God has a plan and a path for our lives but to follow the path takes supernatural strength. That strength is grace! Amazing isn't it??

THE PATH

> ***As arrows are in the hand of a mighty man; so are children of the youth.***
>
> *Psalms 127:4*

This says that children are like arrows in the hand of an archer. If the archer is God and you are the arrow then God must have been aiming at something specific when he released you into the earth. The question is: what was God aiming at when he fired me into the world? Does my life have a purpose and is there a reason for my trials and triumphs? These, of course, are great questions and they were the very questions I asked myself and my audiences wherever I went.

I found out that the word sin means: to miss the mark! Missing your God ordained target in life is the ultimate sin. Missing the very purpose of your existence. You may have guessed it already but I don't think that a lot of the things we call sins are really sins. They may be errors, foolish and even stupid but they are not sins against God. They may be sins against yourself but not against God. If you are going to be scared to sin, then be scared to miss the mark/target that God was aiming at when he fired you into the world. Be scared to live and die having never fulfilled your purpose or realised your full potential. Be scared to pursue a path in life that is incompatible with your purpose in life because this is the ultimate sin...

CHAPTER 3

THE SCHOOL MASTER

I would be lying if I said that I discovered grace through study alone. The fact is that grace is only real to people who have experienced disgrace. Disgrace for me was the feeling of total failure and haunting shame. You see I had crashed, I burned out and nearly lost my mind.

Unfortunately, my personal sense of worth was wrapped up in my ministry. Could you blame me? I had built a large church from scratch and was internationally known as a powerful preacher with a thriving church. Every big name in our group wanted to preach for me and wanted me to preach for them. I had also successfully moved my young family from council housing to a five bed semi in the suburbs. The kids were in private school and two cars were on the drive. I was a hero, an icon and a shining example of dedication and conviction but it was all built on a fault line and a quake was headed my way.

When I decided to follow my new convictions and to lead our large congregation out of legalism, I knew that I risked losing everything including the fame and the fortune. However, when it actually did start falling apart, I literally couldn't handle it. I crumbled as family after family left our church because they didn't like the new direction.

The final straw came in 2003 when a property deal went sour. We attempted to purchase a 3 acre lot on which to purpose-build a new worship centre. The deal fell through because we were unable to complete on the purchase even though we had exchanged contracts and paid a deposit. We couldn't complete the purchase because a last minute survey revealed that the land had been mis-sold to us. It had covenants and restrictions on this potential development that meant it could never be used to build the complex we envisaged. In addition, we learned that other details given to us by the estate agents were false and that the original survey given to us by the agent was likewise falsified. This came as a massive shock because the estate agent was himself a Christian. Our bank was more than willing to finance the purchase at first but when their own survey revealed that it was completely unsuitable for the purposes for which we were buying it; they quite rightly, refused to fund it. We had lost the 10% deposit and any fees paid to architects and consultants. This was money that hard working people had sacrificed to raise.

But more than the financial loss, was the loss of confidence in me as a spiritual leader. You see, these members were not simply following my lead, they were following God in me. When I said; this is a God thing; they believed without question that it had to succeed. The logical conclusion for many of them was that if I was wrong on this project then that's the proof that God is not leading me. Both them and me believed that if God is really in something then it has to work.

Not only did they have questions about my spirituality, but so did I. It felt so right and yet it was so wrong. It looked and sounded like God but how could it be Him in light of this fiasco and how could following 'God' wind up in so much pain and shame? Unfortunately, my understanding of God limited me to that frame. Looking back now, that frame seems so childish and immature on two counts. Firstly, because I do not know of anyone who got it right first time or who didn't experience failure as the school of success. Human beings fail forward and they get wiser as they go. But secondly because, it really is wrong for any man to play God. Today, I would rather say, 'this sounds like a great idea and makes sense to me,' than to say; 'I hear the Lord....'

> ***Surely he hath borne our griefs, and carried our sorrows: yet we did esteem him stricken, smitten of God, and afflicted.***
>
> *Isaiah 53:4*

When Jesus hung on the cross; humiliated, helpless and dying, the people around him reached the same logical conclusion; how could following God end up like this? He can't really be a man of God can he? That is why they concluded that God was in fact punishing Jesus for insolence. The religious frame at the time said; God is good to good people and He is bad to bad people. They could not conceive of bad things happening to good people although they knew that sometimes good things happen to bad people. They even had a Scripture for their interpretation of the cross.

> ***And if a man have committed a sin worthy of death, and he be to be put to death, and thou hang him on a tree: 23] His body shall not remain all night upon the tree, but thou shalt in any wise bury him that day; (for he that is hanged is accursed of God;) that thy land be not defiled, which the LORD thy God giveth thee for an inheritance.***
>
> *Deuteronomy 21:22-23*

To many, this was proof that Jesus was an imposter. Even his disciples didn't envisage this end for a supposedly good man. It was in this frame that many interpreted the collapse of the project I.e. proof that He was an imposter! I really couldn't blame any of them and still don't. You see, my theological frame was still evolving and was at an immature stage. My mistake was to attach the name of God to a commercial venture and then to try and hold God to an outcome. As you will learn from this book, following God may not lead to the outcomes you envisage because the outcomes you envisage may only be the bait that lures you onto a path that is designed to correct and perfect you. Your dream may evaporate before your eyes after you have laboured to materialise it. But that's ok because the value was always in the path. The value is never in what you get. Trust me, the novelty of new things wears off quickly. The value is always in what you are becoming as the result of pursuing your dreams.

In my immaturity and evolving spiritual frame, I made the land purchase a God issue and not a commercial one. Commercial propositions should stand on their merits and make commercial sense. Claims should also be qualified whether they come from a Christian or an atheist. Due diligence all round makes good business sense. But make no mistake; even after you do all that; a commercial venture can still flop and anyone going into one must understand the nature of risk. I know this now but didn't know it then. The secret to personal or business success is the ability to convert failure into feedback and then getting back up again.

> ***For a just man falleth seven times, and riseth up again: but the wicked shall fall into mischief.***
>
> *Proverbs 24:16*

My frame did not understand this principle and couldn't process the collapse of the project. Neither could my flock, who had fed from my fountain of flawed theology.

I will never forget the feeling of shame and disgust in the form of a big knot in my chest, when I stood up to tell the church that the deal had fallen through and that we have lost a lot of money. I was literally devastated, confused, disillusioned and broken. How could I be so wrong, when it felt so right?

The fact that we lost the property, lost the money and lost our hopes, was devastating enough. But what followed made all of that seem like child's play. That year, a number of Christian leaders were publicly scandalised in the media for financial mismanagement among other scandals. Several churches made the mainstream press as their operations came under investigation. At the same time, an anonymous member of my congregation wrote three letters: the first to the charities commission, (government watch dog for charities), the second to the IRS and the third to a news paper. The letter basically said that the pastor has stolen over £100,000 from the church in the name of a scam building project.

I will never forget the call I got from a Journalist eager to publish the story. I think the only reason they didn't publish a story was because I laughed so hard at the allegation. I wasn't worried at all because I never handled any money and also had a clear audit trail. I likewise can't forget the visit I had from the IRS who launched a surprise investigation against me. They sent a specialist unit who specialised in church scandals. Again I came up clean because there was never anything to hide. I also remember telling the charity commissioners to 'Go ahead and investigate everything. I'm not going away and the buck stops with me...so go for it.'

For the next year of my life, I was under investigation and close scrutiny. That was ok because I didn't feel as though I had anything to hide or be ashamed of. What I was not ready for was the impact that all this attention had on my congregation. You see in the same year, 8 of those 10 pastors left me. They sited many things i.e. the new direction, God was leading them on etc. Some just disappeared. Likewise the church split in half and the average attendance came down to 400 from 900.

I know some people think it's childish and unprofessional for a preacher to whine about people leaving, but these were people that I was emotionally connected to. Our church was built on soul winning and although the fault line of legalism was there, the majority of my congregation had converted to Christianity through my ministry. Some were drug addicts, gangsters, prostitutes and the like. I became personally involved with each of them. I did counselling every week, visited them in hospital, paid their rents, married them, blessed their babies, financed the start up of their businesses, buried their parents and grand parents and otherwise provided a genuine pastoral service. I watched many of them grow from drug addicts to home-owning business couples with children. Some of them left without saying bye and others left with spiteful words.

With half a congregation and only two preachers left out of 10 and on half our income, I soldiered on not even realising that I had become clinically depressed.

DEPRESSION

I never knew I was depressed until I read an NHS pamphlet on depression and realised that I had every symptom. I couldn't sleep for days at a time and went to see my GP for help with sleeping. It was while waiting in the surgery that I read the pamphlet. Shocking! I was clinically depressed at a dangerous level.

I couldn't be depressed; I am a preacher for goodness sakes and I had a great sense of humour. I loved a laugh and was generally great company, so how in the world could I be depressed. I thought depressed people couldn't laugh or smile. I thought they were melodramatic people who saw a half empty cup in everything. Boy was I wrong. Depression is a serious medical condition that is usually accompanied by feelings of hopelessness and resignation. At the mild end, it may express itself in reckless and careless behaviour but at the extreme end, it expresses itself in suicide.

I don't remember being suicidal, but the truth was that I wanted to die and didn't mind if it happened today. I would see a hearse drive by and literally envy the person in the back. For peace and quiet I would take a book and go sit on a bench to read. Not a park bench, but a bench in the local cemetery. How morbid was that? But to me it was the most peaceful spot on earth. I finally realised that something was dreadfully wrong when I caught myself praying that I wouldn't make it back from my next trip.

Don't get me wrong, I loved my family but genuinely felt they would be better off without me. I had lost the will to live, the desire to fight and the hope of a better future. Life was dark and there was no light in it for me. My world had collapsed, everything around me was hurting and it was now impossible to repair.

Thankfully my GP diagnosed the condition quickly and prescribed some antidepressant medication for me. So there I was; preaching the gospel and popping antidepressants. Not sure what the medication ultimately achieved but I'm sure it helped if only with the sleeping.

IT GETS WORSE

Of course all of this had a very adverse affect on my marriage which was already struggling. It's hard if not impossible to live a normal life with a depressed person in the house. My short fuse got even shorter, little things seemed big and communicating became nigh impossible. We started to see a professional marriage counselling couple who came highly recommended by a senior church leader. However, in hind sight I think we left it too late. The final round of marriage counselling collapsed in confusion and frustration. Inside I had given up. What no one really knew was that I hadn't just given up on the marriage, I had given up on life itself. I quit believing that the future couldn't hold any sorrow for me.

You see the culture of our churches at the time was very unforgiving when it came to marital breakdowns. You literally had to be married to be credible. A single minister was either gay or a whoremonger. There was no grey. To cap it all, the church I 'got saved in' was dead set against divorce and absolutely anathematised re-marriage. There were even many in my new circle who shared the same point of view. A second marriage was adultery; plain and simple! That is why, even though my marriage was technically over and our differences had become irreconcilable, walking away from it was ministerial suicide. It was unthinkable!

There was no future for me. I had preached all my life, since I was 17 years old. I knew nothing else. So, with a failing church, a failing marriage and a failing mind, all that made sense was going to sleep and never waking up. I had become the person

I preached against. I hated me, blamed me, punished myself and otherwise behaved like a man who wanted to die.

I moved out of my family home and into a small apartment. This tore me apart because it hit my two boys really hard. They were literally the love of my life and the only reason to keep living. How could they possibly process the collapse of their own home. How could they come to terms with daddy and mummy not together? Of course, I only slept in the apartment but spent the days at home being dad. (More about that later). So there I was; ministry collapsed, marriage collapsed, clinically depressed and alone in an apartment praying to die.

I had no idea that dismantling the past was the only way to lay hold of the future. Neither had I noticed this pattern in the Bible.

You see, all the predictions of my religious friends had come to pass. I left the doctrines and my life had collapsed. Was this judgement? Did I miss God? At the time I didn't know. I had no idea that dismantling the past was the only way to lay hold of the future. Neither had I noticed this pattern in the Bible. My dismantling was severe because my religiosity was so intense. My religion had to crash before grace could appear.

Looking back now, it seems so stupid because I was dearly loved and valued by hundreds if not thousands of people. But in my twisted mind; they would all be better off without me.

LEAD ME TO CHRIST

I suppose I'm telling you how a person discovers grace. You never really know it until your religion collapses and your personal efforts fail. The Bible says that the Law was a school master to bring us to Christ. Let's read it:

> ***Wherefore the law was our schoolmaster to bring us unto Christ, that we might be justified by faith. 25 But after that faith is come, we are no longer under a schoolmaster. 26 For ye are all the children of God by faith in Christ Jesus.***
>
> *Galations 3:24-26*

In the original language, the word schoolmaster doesn't refer to a teacher, instead it refereed to the person who took the children to school. Back in those days, rich families employed a school master, whose sole purpose was to make sure the kids get to school safely and on time.

Paul here describes the Laws of Moses as bringing us or in fact dragging us to Christ. It suggests that the law forces us to accept Christ. But why? Because the true purpose of the Law was to conclusively expose our utter inability to perfectly obey instructions from God. It is the revelation of our imperfection that forces us to Christ.

Contrary to the teachings of some; the law was never meant to justify Israel or to generate righteousness. It was meant to generate humility in people who realised that they couldn't keep it. It was meant to expose our inability to justify ourselves and to leave us in need of a Saviour. It was designed to prove that we are no better than Adam or Eve and that we all would have done the same thing in the garden. The law should have humbled Israel; not made her proud. The law was designed to make us sinners; not saints, because only a sinner can accept the gospel of grace.

> ***Now we know that what things soever the law saith, it saith to them who are under the law: that every mouth may be stopped, and all the world may become guilty before God. 20 Therefore by the deeds of the law there shall no flesh be justified in his sight: for by the law is the knowledge of sin.***
>
> *Romans 3:19-20*

So there I was; religion collapsed, alone, depressed and confused, wallowing in failure and shame, when I had a supe natural experience. I realise for some this will appear to be little more than a psychotic episode and you will begin praying for my deliverance from psychosis. However, if this was psychosis, then I highly recommend it to everyone.

SUPERNATURAL VISITATION

One night I was fast asleep when in the early hours of the morning I was woken up by a feeling I was quite used to but hadn't felt in a while. Us Pentecostals call it the anointing, or the presence of the Holy Spirit. It was upon me so thick, covering every inch of my body until it felt like my soul would explode within me. I couldn't shake it off nor sleep it off.

It just got thicker until I started speaking in tongues. So I got up and went to my little living room to pray. While there, it was as though Jesus sat down next to me and began talking with me. His voice was in my mind but it was so clear that it might as well have been audible. To this day I don't know if it was audible or not, I only know that it was so real that there would have been no difference.

We had a conversation that went on for a few hours. I know it sounds bizarre and in light of the state I was in, I would understand if anyone thought this was plain and simple psychosis. But for me, it was real. I can't tell you everything He said, but here is a summary.

He said, 'Wayne, I love you. I have always loved you and will always love you. I found you when you were 15 and knew you before then. I have watched over you your whole life and kept you from many things you didn't even know about. I will never leave you and I've never left you. When you felt like I wasn't there, I was carrying you. You are mine, you are special and I have a plan for your life. Don't give up and keep preaching.'

I interrupted several times with hot tears streaming down my face, 'I can't do it Lord, my life is over, you can't ask me to preach, you know I'll embarrass you, I'm not worthy, just take me and take me now.'

He said, 'I know all there is to know about you. I know your past, present and future and yes I love you. My grace is enough for you and my strength is made perfect in your weakness.'

Well, I proceeded to ask tons of questions like: 'Lord I can't do church as usual. I don't even believe half the stuff I'm supposed to and I don't trust church people. What about me being single? Is there hope for me? Is there a second chance? Will life ever be great again?'

He simply said, 'Wayne, I love YOU'. He then told me a few things I could do and few things I couldn't and the conversation ended. When it did, my whole being was full of love. I could not believe it; I started praying for everyone and anyone I could think of. I had a strange love for all my critics, enemies and anyone that had ever hurt me. I prayed for my estranged wife, my mother, my children and siblings. Cousins and uncles; I just loved everyone. I didn't care if people left me or stayed with me because something had fundamentally changed in me.

TRANSFORMATION

First of all, I knew God was still with me. I knew He loved me unconditionally and that He had fully calculated the risk of using me, a broken man, to preach his word. Secondly I stopped linking my worth to my work. You see, up until that point, I had lost a sense of worth because it was completely linked to my crumbling work. I had also stopped linking my value with my achievements. Warts an all, success or failure, good or bad decisions, I was still a worthwhile human being. God loved me, knowing me better than I know myself. He was on my side, giving me another chance. I found a new love for me and a new love for life. Now I wanted to live and live for as long as possible.

Needless to say, I threw away the antidepressants and was liberated from depression by the revelation of Grace.

CHAPTER 4
THE RAPTURE

Grace brought an awaking to my troubled and tormented soul but it would be years before my theological transformation was complete. When I say complete, I don't mean concluded. I mean that even though I realised that I could no more win God's love than a child could win their parent's love, I still had to make sense of certain passages that posed difficulty for me. A surface reading of the Bible without a sound hermeneutic (rules for interpretation) can drag you right back into legalism and into a fearful relationship with an angry God.

My biggest challenge came from an idea that I held so dear and studied so intensely. It was my flagship teaching and I had become internationally famous for teaching it. In Bible school it's called eschatology. It means the doctrine of future things or of the end times. Most Christians have a definite set of beliefs about how the world will end and about the second coming of Christ. We have beliefs about death, the resurrection, heaven and hell. On top of these, many Christians believe that we are right now living in the last days, at the end of time and that

Jesus is about to return any day now. Global warming, unrest in the middle east, nuclear threats, political unions, a cashless society, famines, earthquakes, diseases and terrorism are all signs of the end for believers who embrace the doctrines of the end time.

Well, I was a prolific end time preacher, preaching week in and week out; get ready because Jesus is coming soon. I taught that Christ will come back in two distinct phases. The first we called the rapture. This was the thief in the night. Christ would literally snatch his followers out of the world in a nano second. You'd look round and we'd be gone. Then would follow, anything from three and a half to seven years (depending on your view point) of unprecedented trouble for the unbelievers left on planet earth. Everything from nuclear holocaust to plagues and a raft of natural disasters. During that period, the anti Christ would become the leader of a new world order and attempt to make devil worship compulsory.

We taught that things would get so bad in that period that only the second phase of Christ's second coming would save the earth from complete destruction. The final phase was that Christ would appear in the sky with the saints He had earlier snatched away just moments before Israel is annihilated at the battle of Armageddon. Sounds detailed doesn't it? And detailed it was. I studied every bit of it, I wrote books on it, published a magazine on it and created a TV show about it. I was synonymous with end time prophesy.

In fact, many of the members of my church came to Christ during one of my 'prophesy crusades'. During those crusades

I would use a projector to show vivid pictures of what was going to happen to people who missed the rapture. I then gave an altar call, which went something like this: 'Dear friend, nothing is more important right now than that you are ready to meet Christ when He comes. He could come tonight and tomorrow might be too late. All the signs are in place, you've got no time to waste. Come to Christ now or spend eternity in a lake of fire with the devil and his demons. Well, what are you waiting for...run...run to Christ before its too late...' And run they did, straight down the aisle to the altar to pray for forgiveness. I had successfully scared them to Christ. I did this unashamedly because of the way I interpreted Scriptures.

> ***Paul said, 'knowing the terror of the Lord, we persuade men..'***
>
> *2 Corinthians 5:11.*

Likewise Jesus said...

> ***For as in the days that were before the flood they were eating and drinking, marrying and giving in marriage, until the day that Noah entered into the ark, 39] And knew not until the flood came, and took them all away; so shall also the coming of the Son of man be. 40] Then shall two be in the field; the one shall be taken, and the other left. 41] Two women shall be grinding at the mill; the one shall be taken, and the other left.***
>
> *Matt 24:38-41*

I had these passages and many others like them guiding my approach to evangelism. I preached it like it was going to happen tonight and people responded immediately. It's no longer a surprise to me that many of those people whom I scared to Christ are no longer with Him. You see, the less I preached on these subjects; the less reason they had to stay. As they say; out of sight, out of mind. Without the rapture, the thief in the night and the eternal fires of hell before them, they simply had no reason to stay.

So I guess you are wondering why I stopped preaching on these subjects and what on earth do I now believe? Good question but let me stick with the journey.

Let me start by making it abundantly clear that at no point did I begin to question the authenticity or inspiration of the Bible. I believe the Bible is given to us by God, through men. Because of that fact, I don't worship the Bible as some fundamentalists do, but neither do I take a jot or title away from its inspired pages. It is God breathed and Divinely inspired. The whole book is written FOR us; but none of it is written TO us. This means that you have to interpret it in its historic context and then draw inspiration, application and revelation from that point of view.

Many preachers still lift passages out of Jeremiah and insist that this is God's word to us all. Well preacher; you are wrong! It was God's word to them at that time. It is only God's word to us in a metaphoric sense. This error undergirds legalism to the full. It is precisely why we preached against jewellery, make up, women wearing trousers and the like. Because the Bible said it! The problem is that the Bible never said it to us. It said it to them. The question is; why and what can we learn from it? It is a fundamental flaw made by most fundamentalists to convert historic lessons into present day edicts.

> ***'Now all these things happened unto them for examples: and they are written for our admonition, upon whom the ends of the world are come.'***
>
> *1 Corinthians 10:11*

According to Paul, God made sure that things got written down so we could learn something from it. It was not written to us but for us.

So back to my point, I never questioned the authenticity or inspiration of the Bible, however I did begin to question my interpretation of it for a few good reasons as follows:

I noticed that our children and young people were not doing well at school. At the time, I didn't even see the obvious link between my teaching and the death of aspiration. When I asked a few of them what the problem was, they replied, 'Why work hard at school when Jesus is coming back any day now?' Wow! Talk about a child teaching you something. It happened to me that day. These children were stating the obvious; there was no sense aspiring to anything in life if the Antichrist is going to get it all and Jesus is going to snatch us out of here tonight... possibly!

Of course I was defensive and tried to explain that we should keep busy until Jesus comes and shouldn't just stop when we think He is coming. But the truth was still eating away at my soul. I had convinced these kids that they had no future and among them were my own kids. I really struggled here and attempted to explain myself but it was too late. The haunting truth was that an imminent rapture was totally incompatible with a productive future. This was a blow to say the least because this was my flagship message.

I decided to go back to the scriptures for a more balanced point of view, because at no point did I want young people to opt out of society...

I decided to go back to the Scriptures for a more balanced point of view, because at no point did I want young people to opt out of society, but this was precisely the effect that my message was having on them. So I did and what I discovered was not only life changing, but it has come to characterise my ministry today. Thankfully today, my name is synonymous with aspiration but that was not always the case.

In order to explain my findings, I will have to go deep. I.e. get theological. But don't worry because I really think this is the last chapter on theology. Here goes:

The Bible took on new meaning for me when my hermeneutics (method of interpretation) changed. For example, when it comes to prophecy, most people think that a prophecy is written in Scripture to help us predict the future. Fortunately; they are wrong! The purpose of the prophecy is always to help us interpret the past. Believe it or not, your past requires more interpretation than does your future. After all it is your past that's preventing you from seizing the future right now.

About a third of the Bible is made up of futuristic prophecies, most of which have already been fulfilled in the first coming of Christ at Bethlehem. They are called messianic prophecies because they identify Jesus as the long awaited Messiah. For example, the place of his birth is foretold in Micah 5:2

But thou, Bethlehem Ephratah, though thou be little among the thousands of Judah, yet out of thee shall he come forth unto me that is to be ruler in Israel; whose goings forth have been from of old, from everlasting.

The fact that He would go into Egypt was predicted in Hosea 11:1 When Israel was a child, then I loved him, and called my son out of Egypt. The fact that He would grow up in Nazareth is then predicted in Judges 13:5

For, lo, thou shalt conceive, and bear a son; and no razor shall come on his head: for the child shall be a Nazarite unto God from the womb: and he shall begin to deliver Israel out of the hand of the Philistines.

Please note, I am not the one saying that these passages point to Jesus, it is Matthew in his gospel who lifts these passages out of the Old Testament and says they point to Christ. Let's look at Matthew 2:1-6.

> ***Now when Jesus was born in Bethlehem of Judea in the days of Herod the king, behold, there came wise men from the east to Jerusalem, 2] Saying, Where is he that is born King of the Jews? for we have seen his star in the east, and are come to worship him. 3] When Herod the king had heard these things, he was troubled, and all Jerusalem with him. 4] And when he had gathered all the chief priests and scribes of the people together, he demanded of them where Christ should be born. 5] And they said unto him, In Bethlehem of Judea: for thus it is written by the prophet, 6] And thou Bethlehem, in the land of Judah, art not the least among the princes of Judah: for out of thee shall come a Governor, that shall rule my people Israel.***

Matthew here says that Micah 5:2 identified the place of Christ's birth. Let's continue:

> ***When he arose, he took the young child and his mother by night, and departed into Egypt: 15] And was there until the death of Herod: that it might be fulfilled which was spoken of the Lord by the prophet, saying, Out of Egypt have I called my son.***
>
> *Matthew 2:14-15*

Here is the Egypt Prophecy being fulfilled. And finally the Nazareth prophecy..

And he came and dwelt in a city called Nazareth: that it might be fulfilled which was spoken by the prophets, He shall be called a Nazarene.

Matthew 2:23

Ok, here is the dilemma: When you read the actual prophesies themselves, it is absolutely impossible to predict where Christ would be born, when He would go to Egypt or that He would grow up in Nazareth. Matthew does not use these prophesies to predict the future. He uses them to interpret the past. It is only post the event that the prophesies make sense. But before the event they are simply confusing. Anyone trying to make predictions based on these prophesies would have speculated and would have been wrong.

For we know in part, and we prophesy in part.
10] But when that which is perfect is come,
then that which is in part shall be done away.
11] When I was a child, I spake as a child,
I understood as a child, I thought as a child:
but when I became a man, I put away child-
ish things. 12] For now we see through a glass,
darkly; but then face to face: now I know in
part; but then shall I know even as also
I am known.

1 Corinthians 13:9-12

Paul here teaches that a futuristic prophesy is like looking through dark window. You don't fully know what you are looking at but when it arrives; then you will know!

The fact is that Jesus was born in Bethlehem; He escaped to Egypt and grew up in Nazareth. Only after that sequence of events did three unrelated and obscure passages in the Old Testament make any sense at all. In fact most of those OT passages have a primary historic meaning that has nothing to do with a future Christ. It is only post the events that a secondary metaphoric and prophetic meaning was given to these passages.

Put simply, if you use Biblical prophecies to predict the future, you will come up with pure speculation and probably be totally wrong, because those prophesies will only ever make sense post the events. Matthew simply looked back at the events and said, 'Ah, this is what the Scripture meant when it said...' Likewise Peter at Pentecost does not quote Joel before the Holy Spirit arrives but after the event he says, 'Ah, this is that which was spoken by the prophet Joel.'

When I understood this principle, I realised that I had to stop predicting what was going to happen. Instead; I had to listen to Jesus more carefully:

> ***But of that day and hour knoweth no man, no, not the angels of heaven, but my Father only.***
>
> *Matthew 24:36*

> ***Watch therefore: for ye know not what hour your Lord doth come. 43] But know this, that if the goodman of the house had known in what watch the thief would come, he would have watched, and would not have suffered***

> ***his house to be broken up. 44] Therefore be ye also ready: for in such an hour as ye think not the Son of man cometh.***
>
> *Matthew 24:42-44*

Scripture is quite clear about this simple fact; no one knows when Jesus will come back. The only thing we do know is that it will be totally unexpected. Jesus was coming back when I was 17 and now I'm 45 He is still coming soon. That's almost 30 years of watching the news, reading the signs and waiting for the thief in the night. I don't want to sound cynical here because I deeply believe that Christ will return. My cynicism is aimed at the prophecy teachers who keep us on the edge of our seats.

When Jesus was asked by his disciples what the signs of his coming would be, He proceeded to tell them about false prophets, wars, famines, earthquakes and diseases. I always thought that these were signs of the end, but Jesus said:

> ***see that ye be not troubled: for all these things must come to pass, but the end is not yet. 7] For nation shall rise against nation, and kingdom against kingdom: and there shall be famines, and pestilences, and earthquakes, in divers places. 8] All these are the beginning of sorrows.***
>
> *Matthew 24:6-8*

He never said that these were signs of the end but rather that they were the beginning of sorrows. In the original language, the word sorrows means 'birth pains' or contractions. As every mother knows, contractions increase with frequency and intensity as the moment of birth draws near. They are designed to push out the NEW THING, that has been hidden in the womb. These global contractions were meant to signify the soon arrival of something new.

I realised that everything I taught to be a sign of the end was in fact a sign of the beginning. Now of course an end is a beginning and a beginning is an end. But clearly our focus is not supposed to be the end. Our focus is meant to be the beginning.

What are you saying Bishop? It's very simple: there is no such thing in the Bible as an end of the world. I understand why a surface reading of the Scriptures, without a sound hermeneutic and reliable study tools, would lead someone to conclude that the end is nigh. However, the Greek word translated 'world' in these passages means 'age' or 'era'. It is the age that will end, not planet earth.

> ***One generation passeth away, and another generation cometh: but the earth abideth for ever.***
>
> *Eccl 1:4*

The earth is going nowhere, but the age is going to end. Many Christians are scared to talk about a New Age. They are scared that they will be accused of joining the New Age movement with its metaphysics, crystals, tarot cards, the occult and its age of aquarius. Well I'm certainly not for all that, but I am for reclaiming our kingdom vocabulary. You see the New Age is Biblical. It is what the Bible means by: a new heaven and a new earth. These are not new by creation, but they are new by cleansing and regeneration.

The end time message is really an expression of the gospel of the Kingdom. It announces that God will finally purge the planet and bring an end to strife. And guess what? Jesus only gave one sign for the end of the age:

> ***And this gospel of the Kingdom shall be preached in all the world for a witness to all nations and then shall the end come.***
>
> *Matthew 24:14*

The witness to all nations is the only sign of the end given by Jesus in Matthew 24. But please look deeper with me. The word gospel means good news. My question is; who are these people that have the gall to preach good news in the face of global turbulence? Who would dare demonstrate extreme optimism when the news headlines are full of fear? Well, they would have to be a very special breed of believers to suggest that something good is on the horizon. Secondly, please notice that the bearers of good news are not trying to escape; they are seeking to invade the world. According to Jesus they will be in all the world preaching until every nation has proof. So the true sign of the end of the age is the appearance of a unique people, who are optimistic in their outlook and unafraid to go into every aspect of the world's system in order to be ambassadors of hope.

I realised that my message fell short. You see, I had no good news for the world. I was not an optimist. I was a pessimist and my ministry thrived on pessimism. I began to see that both my children and I may be around for a lot longer than I had previously predicted and that I had to inspire aspiration and optimism in them and me. The kids had to do well at school and people had to plan on being here a lot longer than expected.

Well Bishop, have you done away with all your prophecy teachings? What about all the stuff you taught on Israel, the third Temple, the anti-Christ and the mark of the beast? Well it's simple. I now understand that these references are metaphors with meanings that transcend times and culture. Every generation has had its own Antichrist, mark of the beast and the like. Likewise; the last days have been with us since the day of Pentecost.

> ***Little children, it is the last time: and as ye have heard that antichrist shall come, even now are there many antichrists; whereby we know that it is the last time.***
>
> *1 John 2:18*

You simply could not tell the Christians that were being branded and burned at the stake by the Roman Emperor Nero, that the book of Revelation had anything to do with anyone but them. It has multiple applications to multiple generations and circumstances. The overall message being that in the end, we win!!!

Oh, I still watch the news closely because like previous generations we too are dealing with our own end times.

CHAPTER 5
THE INVASION

As an end time preacher, I was fundamentally an escapist who preached a mass evacuation of planet earth by the saints. By saints, I meant those who were baptised correctly and keeping the rules. Christ would come like a thief in the night and snatch us away before things got too bad. Our main responsibility as Christians was to live right. Living right meant practising separation from the world. We called this holiness. We didn't dress, talk, act or behave like the world. We were never quite sure what that term meant though. 'The world' was anything that wasn't like us.

However, I was undergoing a tumultuous review of my position when it came to the end times. Tumultuous because I had built my ministry on this cherished Christian doctrine. If any of you watch Christian TV, you will soon notice that this idea of a mass evacuation still pervades and undergirds a lot of Christian teaching. However, I was beginning to see things differently.

I was particularly drawn to the message of the seventh angel in Revelation.

> ***And the seventh angel sounded; and there were great voices in heaven, saying, The kingdoms of this world are become the kingdoms of our Lord, and of his Christ; and he shall reign for ever and ever.***
>
> *Revelation 11:15*

I thought about it long and hard. How does a kingdom of this world become a Kingdom of our Lord? The passage appeared to imply that the world as we know it is made up of kingdoms and that these kingdoms would one day be taken over by the Lord. Would this happen in the hereafter or in the here and now? The thought of this happening in the hereafter didn't make sense as I did not believe that any kingdoms of the world would exist in the hereafter. It also was inconsistent with my millennium doctrine as that seemed to happen much later on in Revelation. This had to be a reference to something that would happen this side of eternity and chronologically (based on the time sequence) before the mark of the beast passage or the fall of Babylon the great. Could it have present day implications? Was God planning a take over??

The Penny finally dropped when I heard a preacher preaching a message about the parable of the wheat and the tares. You know the story about wheat and weeds coexisting in the same field. They were so related that anyone trying to separate them would destroy the wheat with the weeds. Only the angels could separate them and the separation would only happen at the end of the age.

I used to think that this passage was describing the condition of the church. There are wheat and weeds in the church but let God sort it out. That was the gist of our thinking at the time. However, Jesus himself explained what the parable meant to his disciples as follows:.

> ***Then Jesus sent the multitude away, and went***
> ***into the house: and his disciples came unto***
> ***him, saying, Declare unto us the parable of the***
> ***tares of the field. 37] He answered and said***
> ***unto them, He that soweth the good seed is***
> ***the Son of man; 38] The field is the world; the***
> ***good seed are the children of the kingdom; but***
> ***the tares are the children of the wicked one;***
> ***39] The enemy that sowed them is the dev-***
> ***il; the harvest is the end of the world; and the***
> ***reapers are the angels. 40] As therefore the***
> ***tares are gathered and burned in the fire; so***
> ***shall it be in the end of this world. 41] The Son***
> ***of man shall send forth his angels, and they***
> ***shall gather out of his kingdom all things that***
> ***offend, and them which do iniquity; 42] And***
> ***shall cast them into a furnace of fire: there***
> ***shall be wailing and gnashing of teeth. 43]***
> ***Then shall the righteous shine forth as the sun***
> ***in the kingdom of their Father. Who hath ears***
> ***to hear, let him hear.***
>
> *Matthew 13:36-43*

Please remember that a parable is really a parallel or a metaphor for something more substantial. The Kingdom is like...not the kingdom is....So here we have some powerful metaphors for which Jesus is giving the keys for correct interpretation.

The preacher took me somewhere I had never been. In fact, he turned my world upside down with his simple sermon when he said...

'The field is not the church brethren, the field is the world! God plants people in the world and they are so connected with the weeds that you better not try to separate them.'

The penny dropped; the thing I had been searching for and my life began to change dramatically. You see, I love studying the good book and I know that for every principle in the Bible, there is also a pattern. In other words, you test the principle by the pattern. If the principle is authentic then the Bible will contain many examples of that principle at work. At that stage you have both a principle and a pattern. When you find a PRINCIPLE and then validate it with a PATTERN, what you now have is a PROMISE, because the principle is typically immutable and unchanging. No pattern, no principle; no principle, no pattern.

The preacher introduced me to a principle and the patterns began to leap out of Scripture. Are there any examples in Scripture of God planting his people in worldly systems? Absolutely. A careful study of Joseph, Nehemiah, Esther and Daniel will reveal an ancient pattern and formula for taking over a kingdom. The Scriptures are filled with accounts of the kingdoms of this world becoming the Kingdoms of our Lord, many times over and the pattern in every case is the same.

JOSEPH

Joseph was the beloved son of Jacob who was sold into slavery by his own brothers. Once in Egypt, Joseph was falsely accused and sentenced to life in prison. In prison he interpreted a dream for which he was eventually remembered by the Pharaoh's butler and the day came when he would interpret the dreams of the mighty Pharaoh himself. Joseph became a father figure to Pharaoh and effectively governed the Kingdom of Egypt. His positioning in a worldly system was the key to Israel's survival and success. Remember, his family was only about 70 souls when they eventually relocated to Egypt, but when they left some 400 years later they numbered in the millions.

What was it that caused Israel's family to multiply into the millions? The strategic positioning of one man in a worldly system!

NEHEMIAH

Nehemiah is famous for rebuilding the broken walls of Jerusalem, however he did it from a strategic position. He was in fact the cup-bearer to King Artaxerxes of Persia. This meant that he had the distinct and royal privilege of serving the King's wine. This was a trusted post because the popular way to assassinate a king in the ancient world was through poisoning. Nehemiah was trusted with the life of a worldly king and would regularly taste his wine before serving it. This clearly meant a lot to the king because in many respects, the fact that Nehemiah was still alive meant that the King would not die from poisoned wine. The king loved him and trusted him completely.

It was in fact the King who noted Nehemiah's sad face and asked what the problem was. This suggests that Nehemiah's regular countenance was cheerful. Can you imagine it; a spiritual man, serving a worldly king with joy? Well the rest of the story is that the King gave him the permit and resources necessary to rebuild the walls of Jerusalem. This strategic kingdom manoeuvre was made possible because a child of God, served God in the kingdoms of men.

ESTHER

Esther was the Jewess who married a Persian King and saved her people from genocide by pleading with her secular husband. She risked her life to plea for a people who had been sentenced to death. It was really mission impossible because the extermination of the Jews was, by this time, enshrined in the laws of the Meades and Persians. The Meades and Persians were very proud of their legal system to the point that once something was written in their law, it could not be altered. Esther dared to ask for the impossible. The result was that her people were saved and the conspirators were executed.

Most Christians believe that Esther's intercession is a metaphor for the church interceding with God for the salvation of souls. However nothing could be further from the truth. First of all, God does not need convincing to save the world. He loves the world more than you or I and has already given his own son for their salvation. No sense praying that God will save the world because He is already determined to do just that. Secondly, the King in this story is not a befitting metaphor for God. He is a pagan King and one that was easily deceived by Haman the antisemitic conspirator. God is not a pagan, neither can He be deceived.

The reason why many Christians interpret the story as Esther = church, the King = God and Haman = the devil, is because they don't understand the principle and the pattern that I am writing about now. The fact is that Esther married a pagan king, who represents secular systems and worldly power. She had no idea that God would use her strategic position to save her people from certain destruction.

DANIEL

Daniel is the prophet who served King Darius the Meade in the courts and kingdom of Babylon. He was a child of the captivity that served God in the kingdoms of men. Daniel enjoyed a beautiful relationship with the king who loved and respected him. He was eventually promoted to the highest political office in Babylon, next to the throne and facilitated the return of the Jews from captivity. He was a praying man and a prophetic man, yet he served God in the political kingdoms of men.

WHAT DO THESE FOUR HAVE IN COMMON?

Firstly they were all bilingual. This means that they spoke two languages; Hebrew and gentile languages. They spoke to God and to each other in Hebrew, but when addressing their pagan friends they spoke the language of the land. Secondly they were all culturally concealed. This means that you couldn't tell from their appearance that they were Hebrews. They would have to tell you or you would have to know their story. Joseph for example, had to unveil himself to his own brothers before they could even recognise him. From the outside he simply looked like an Egyptian prince. Likewise, Esther was ceremonially prepared for her marriage to the king and would have looked like a Persian woman. Not even the King knew that she was really Jewish.

It appears that when God wants to take over a kingdom, he starts by positioning insulated individuals in it.

Finally they each practised insulation, not isolation. When I was an escapist, preaching the great evacuation, my message served to isolate people from the world. People dare not mix with the world and definitely had no aspirations to infiltrate their systems. We practised isolation as though God wanted us to walk on the other side of the street. However Jesus said:

> ***Behold, I send you forth as sheep in the midst of wolves: be ye therefore wise as serpents, and harmless as doves.***
>
> *Matthew 10:16*

True separation from the world is insulation, not isolation. We were obsessed with getting out when God was sending us in.

When I think of Joseph, Nehemiah, Esther and Daniel, I see in them both a pattern and a principle. It appears that when God wants to take over a kingdom, He starts by positioning insulated individuals in it. He then gives them favour with the King and promotes them to a position of power. They then use their influence to advance the Kingdom of God. They are bilingual, culturally concealed and gifted with grace for that space.

I think of them as amphibious creatures who can live in two realms. Not land and sea, but secular and sacred. They are simply comfortable in both. Hopefully you noted in these stories that these individuals were always sent ahead of their people. It's simply not possible to get everyone to see or understand the nature of covert kingdom operations. It is typically individuals who are selected as special agents for the task at hand. They are then given grace for that space and the power to prosper in that field. The others simply catch up to these futuristic forerunners.

ROLES & RECOGNITION

This teaching is difficult for many believers whose highest aspiration is a position in their local church. Many do not feel part of a church in which they cannot serve. They think that their ministry or role in life is church-related and struggle with me because I will not appoint them to a grand church office. The appetite for recognition in the church world is rife. I have seen immature Christians move from church to church in search of titles and recognition. I even observed several of our own members join another church less than 10 minutes away, citing that they weren't getting any where at our church.

The next time I saw them, the majority of them were wearing clergy collars. Their new leader had ordained them as ministers. This insatiable appetite for titles, roles and recognition in the local church is obscuring the true nature of a Christian's calling.

You are fundamentally called to a position in society and not to a position in your church. Of course you should volunteer service to your local church but please don't make the mistake of thinking that that is your great calling. Your higher calling has to do with a position in society to affect change for the Kingdom of God.

If your church needs you; then volunteer your time, talent and treasure to advance the work. If it does not need you right now, then don't get mad and leave. Instead, you should consider the possibility that your gifts and callings are reserved for a secular space.

THE JOSEPH PROPHECY

I am particularly moved by the prophesy that Jacob gave to Joseph just moments before his decease.

> ***22] Joseph is a fruitful bough, even a fruit-***
> ***ful bough by a well; whose branches run over***
> ***the wall: 23] The archers have sorely grieved***
> ***him, and shot at him, and hated him: 24] But***
> ***his bow abode in strength, and the arms of his***
> ***hands were made strong by the hands of the***
> ***mighty God of Jacob; (from thence is the shep-***
> ***herd, the stone of Israel:) 25] Even by the God***
> ***of thy father, who shall help thee; and by the***
> ***Almighty, who shall bless thee with blessings***
> ***of heaven above, blessings of the deep that***
> ***lieth under, blessings of the breasts, and***
> ***of the womb: 26] The blessings of thy father***

> ***have prevailed above the blessings of my progenitors unto the utmost bound of the everlasting hills: they shall be on the head of Joseph, and on the crown of the head of him that was separate from his brethren.***
>
> *Genesis 49:22-26*

Notice that he likened Joseph to a fruitful vine whose branch had gone over the wall. The wall he refers to is the psychological and cultural wall that sits between spiritual people of faith and the world at large. Notice that the well was on this side of the wall but his fruitful branches ran over the wall. This is a beautiful and poetic way of saying that Joseph's roots are in his faith but his fruits are in the world. He was speaking about Joseph's influence in the kingdom of Egypt. This prophecy concludes with bountiful blessings on the head of Joseph.

The great news is that Joseph is not just a person; he is the personification of a principle for which there is a clear pattern. Let me explain:

Joseph was able to save his family from a famine because of his influence in the kingdom of Egypt. But that's Old Testament right? Are there any examples in the New Testament of someone saving the church because of their position in a worldly system? Well, in a metaphoric sense there really is. You see, when Jesus was crucified, according to Roman law, his body should have been thrown onto a bonfire of burning corpses. However He was given a decent burial under Roman guard and seal in a freshly carved tomb. How was that possible? It happened because Nicodemus, a member of the Jewish supreme court and Joseph of Aramathea, a rich man with economic clout, negotiated the deal with Pontius Pilate. Two believers, positioned strategically in the systems of men, saved the BODY OF CHRIST!! Can you see the pattern now?

The good news gets even better. Joseph is not just a person, but a principle, a pattern and a plan. He personifies extraordinary people of faith who dare to invade the secular systems of the world, to use their gifts and abilities there. He represents believers in the system. By system I mean the various components that make up a society I.e. Politics, education, media, entertainment, business, religion and community.

That's when I saw it.... God wants to plant believers in the system. Believers in politics, education, media, entertainment, business, religion and community. From that position they can advance the Kingdom. Wow! Instead of a great evacuation, we were on the verge of a great invasion.

CHAPTER 6

DISCOVERING THE KINGDOM

I was discovering the Kingdom and sincerely thought that the church would see the light and move with me in the new wave. Boy was I wrong. When I first started preaching these truths, it was as though the aliens had landed. What is he on? First the evacuation, now the invasion. He's gone off the rails.

To cap it all, I had just discovered professional coaching as a tool for managing change. There was nothing mystical about it; it was simply a way of achieving clarity about what was important to you and then setting goals and mapping out a plan to attain them. I had successfully used some of the techniques with some young people who were in and out of detention centres and otherwise couldn't keep out of trouble. I would use my coaching techniques to help them create a compelling future for themselves and then to set realistic goals. We would then map out a way forward plan and I would stick with them while they worked the plan, providing added motivation and accountability.

The results were amazing; lives transformed, people making progress and tangible breakthroughs began to appear. So here I was; the guy who used to preach separation from the world and a great evacuation; preaching an invasion and operating as a life coach. People just didn't get it. Wayne Malcolm calls himself a life coach and is helping people with their careers. This, for many, was proof that I had finally lost the plot and gone off the rails. I was asked one Sunday after a sermon, what connection if any I thought my sermon had with Jesus or the gospel. I laughed and asked them to buy the tape, listen to it again where they would find over 40 verses of Scripture quoted verbatim.

People had serious doubts about my new direction and felt that it was not churchy enough. It seemed to be more here and now than it was there and then. It didn't seem to emphasise consecration, conviction, repentance and separation from the world. It was an anything goes message with no rules to even regulate. They were uncomfortable and understandably so, considering where we had come from. It was as though people didn't want a practical solution to a problem, they wanted a spiritual and mystical one. They wanted a miracle; not a methodology. Of course they wanted a better quality of life but they would achieve this by miracles. To suggest a methodology would imply that they could do it without God and they simply did not want it without Him because that would make them no different to the sinner.

I remember being asked to explain the difference between Christian and secular self-development. The person felt that self development was a secular substitute for spiritual growth and that my teaching was nothing more than heresy. It was bringing the world into the church and the church into the world. Honestly, I was the alien who had landed. Over the years my vocabulary became foreign to churchy people as were my ideas. I was out on a limb and had no idea that that was where all the fruits were.

THE KINGDOM IS...

It all made sense when I realised that there is a big difference between the Kingdom of God and the church of God and that trying to get the church to see Kingdom things was like asking a child to operate a crane. It was way beyond the scope of our theology and world view. The kingdom didn't really make sense to us because we thought it simply was the church. Getting folks into the kingdom meant getting them into church. The kingdom in action was the church in action. We used the words kingdom and church synonymously and interchangeably. This was wrong because the kingdom is much bigger than the church and is always chronologically ahead of the church so that the church is forever catching up to where the kingdom already is. Let me explain and then prove it with some Biblical patterns.

A minister who had become aware of some kingdom things said to me, 'Wayne how are we going to get the church to see these things and become a dynamic force for change in the world?' I answered, 'We're not.' 'Aren't you going to try?' I said, 'No.' He said, 'Why not?' I said, 'Because the church will eventually catch up to where the Kingdom already is. My job is to prepare some resources that will help them out when the penny finally drops.'

I explained to him that the church is always chronologically behind the kingdom and is always playing catch up.

I showed him that the Kingdom reached Cornelius' house before the church did. When Peter got there in Acts 10, God was already there. In fact God had more trouble persuading the church to go to Cornelius than He did getting Cornelius to embrace the church. The kingdom went ahead of the church and paved the way for it. This reminds me of Jospeh in Egypt. The Kingdom was there before Joseph's brothers got there. God went ahead of them and paved the way. Can you believe it? The kingdom was at work in Egypt long before the 'church' of that day got there. Hopefully you can see the pattern.

The Kingdom was at work in unlikely places like the palaces of Kings, dungeons and dens, while the church had no idea that the kingdom was there. The church would eventually catch up to the Kingdom but only after a path was paved. That's why individuals who are kingdom people appear as aliens to churchy people. They are simply ahead of their time and a represent a voice from the future.

The Kingdom is not the church, neither is the church the kingdom although one is inside of the other. A Kingdom is literally a Kings domain. It is the realm over which he rules. God's Kingdom is his domain, his realm, his territory, his influence. It is spiritual in nature and everlasting in scope. It is inside the believer and the believer is inside of it.

Fundamentally, the Kingdom of God is the influence of God. Whenever you see God influencing the affairs of men, that is the Kingdom at work. Influence is a powerful word. It means: the capacity or power of persons or things to be a compelling force on or produce effects on the actions, behaviour, opinions, etc., of others:.

According to this definition, influence is the power to produce effects on the actions, behaviour and opinions of others. God's influence is the compelling force which affects the opinions and actions of men. Whenever this occurs in the Bible or in society, the Kingdom is at work.

The church on the other hand is comprised of people who respond to the call of the gospel. The word literally means the called, or the Assembly of God. Historically the word describes a town cryer calling the residents of the town to an assembly at the town hall. Those who responded were called, the church, the assembly, the called. In this respect, the church of Jesus began at Pentecost in Acts 2, but the Kingdom of God was here aeons before Pentecost. The Kingdom is broader and includes any territory controlled by God. It includes people and institutions over which God is reigning.

The Kingdom is broader and includes any territory controlled by God.

The church is in the Kingdom and the Kingdom is in the church for one simple reason: everyone in it has come under the INFLUENCE OF GOD. However, there are many people who are not in the church but are under the INFLUENCE OF GOD. For example, no one in the old testament was part of the

New Testament church, yet they were part of the Kingdom because they were under the INFLUENCE OF GOD. It is also true that many of the pagan Kings in the Old Testament operated under the INFLUENCE OF GOD. These include the Pharaoh, King Ahasuerus, King Artaxerxes, King Nebuchadnezzar, King Darius and others. In fact God even referred to a pagan King, Cyrus, as His anointed servant.

This is really difficult for many believers to accept that Jesus has sheep of another fold.

> ***I am the good shepherd, and know my sheep,***
> ***and am known of mine. 15] As the Father***
> ***knoweth me, even so know I the Father: and***
> ***I lay down my life for the sheep. 16 And other***
> ***sheep I have, which are not of this fold: them***
> ***also I must bring, and they shall hear my voice;***
> ***and there shall be one fold, and one shepherd.***
>
> *John 10:14-16*

DO YOU REMEMBER THIS STORY ALSO:

> ***And John answered him, saying, Master, we***
> ***saw one casting out devils in thy name, and he***
> ***followeth not us: and we forbade him, because***
> ***he followeth not us. 39] But Jesus said, Forbid***
> ***him not: for there is no man which shall do a***
> ***miracle in my name, that can lightly speak evil***
> ***of me. 40] For he that is not against us is on***
> ***our part. 41] For whosoever shall give you***
> ***a cup of water to drink in my name,***

> ***because ye belong to Christ, verily I say unto you, he shall not lose his reward.***
>
> *Mark 9:38-41*

This one is deep because it implies that anyone helping the mission is part of the mission and will be rewarded for their part.

Many people unknowingly play a part in God's great plan. They do it because they are under the INFLUENCE OF GOD and are part of the Kingdom in action. Many Christians still write off non Christians who are clearly under the INFLUENCE OF GOD and are delivering much needed aide, support and resources, for healing and helping vulnerable people because their theology doesn't make room for the Kingdom in action.

May I remind you that Jesus preached the gospel of the Kingdom and not the gospel of the church. He only mentions the church twice but the Kingdom is always the crux of his message. His miracles were all demonstrations or illustrations of the Kingdom in action. This is what made Jesus such a revolutionary character. His words suggested that a higher Kingdom than that of Rome was present in Him and in all who believe. He turned people on to the idea that God was running things, not Rome, not the Sanhedrin, not Herod and not the Pharisees. God was systematically repossessing planet earth for his own glory and bringing in a new age of peace. The difference was that the new age started within. You must first find the kingdom within before you can see it without.

AHEAD OF MY TIME

At the time of writing this book, I am pretty popular on the preaching circuit. I preach for a variety of ministries and organisations at their conferences and special events right across the spectrum of Christendom. Although the Christian community is still quite segregated along cultural, ethnic and denominational lines, I still get invited to speak for majority white groups, African groups and Caribbean ones too. On each occasion, I get raving reviews from my hosts and from the crowds. Revelatory, cutting edge, revolutionary are the words I have become familiar with when leaving a venue.

Sometimes it has brought me to tears listening to the testimonials of my hosts about the effect my words have had on their ministry. Some felt as though it completely revolutionised their outlook and approach to mission or doing church. I even had a popular TV minister, nearly twice my age, who has been preaching longer than I have been alive, tell me that in all his years he has never heard so much revelation come out of the mouth of one man. Of course I was deeply humbled. But what he and the many others did not know is that all those sermons are over 10 years old. I first preached them to my struggling church over a decade ago, only to be greeted like an alien from outer space. They didn't get it then, but people get it now.

A pioneer is seldom celebrated by his own generation. It is typically the next generation who benefits from their life's work. Their own generation is usually nervous, intimidated, scared or confused by a new burst of light. They can't handle the implications of change and so choose to crucify it before it grows up.

THE NEXT MOVE

The next move of God in your life has no greater enemy than the last one. So said one of my chief mentors who helped me make the transition from religion to relationship and from doctrines to metaphors. He shared with me how grace had no worse enemy than the law and that those who cleaved to the law were the chief opponents of grace. The dilemma is that both came from God.

I quickly identified a Biblical pattern for this principle. For example, do you remember the manna that fell from heaven and sustained the children of Israel for forty years in the wilderness? Of course you do. Each day the children of Israel would wake up to a fresh supply of manna. That was until some smart Alex decided to take up two days worth in one day. I guess they figured that they could have a long lie in tomorrow. However when they went to the pot on the next day, the manna had gone off. Well the Bible puts it a little stronger than that. It stank and had worms in it. Now how is it possible that something which came from God could stink and and become worm infested? The answer is simple; it was good for the day in which it was sent but you can't live today off yesterday's manna.

JESUS SAID:

> ***...It is written, Man shall not live by bread alone, but by every word that proceedeth out of the mouth of God.***
>
> *Matthew 4:4*

That word 'proceedeth' implies the present tense. In other words, our spiritual life is linked to our ability to hear what God is presently or currently saying. The problem is that what God is currently saying may in fact be diametrically opposed to what He previously said. This does not mean that God contradicts himself but rather that He chooses to manifest his purposes in stages. Each stage has its own word that was good for then but may not be good for now. For example, the same God who told Abraham to kill Isaac, then told him not to do it. The test was a necessary part of Abraham's development as a Father of faith. Could you imagine what would have happened if Abraham stubbornly cleaved to the first instruction? What if he said to himself; 'God wouldn't contradict himself, I'm gonna hold fast to the first word, I'm not moving, I'm not changing.' What would have happened? He would have killed his own son, doing exactly what God told him to do all because he was stuck on a word.

What is God now saying for this season of your life? Even if it contradicts what He said, are you willing like Abraham to exercise some 'NOW FAITH'. The kingdom is calling you into the future but you will have to let go of the past. As painful as that may sound, please know that the will of God will never take you where the grace of God cannot keep you.

People of faith have a well documented propensity to idolise the past. However the Kingdom is a voice from the future. You have to look forward and trust that God is taking you along the pathways of destiny.

CHAPTER 7

GRACE FOR MY SPACE

I had become a Kingdom man with a Kingdom message. I was now concerned with politics, economics, social justice and equal opportunities. I thought about education, jobs, housing and of course our failing youth culture. The city became my parish and the local church my base. In the past, the local church was the be all and end all of my calling but now the city, the nation and the world itself was a whole new mission field. Social institutions, big corporations and political parties were no longer something God wanted us out of but rather something He wanted us into. My message had changed, my tone had changed, my ministry had changed and so had my personality.

As I became more kingdom, I became less churchy. Instead of praise the Lord brother, it became Hi Joe. Instead of introducing my self as Bishop Wayne Malcolm, I would simply say, my name is Wayne. My very vocabulary changed as I began to enjoy having normal conversations with ordinary people of different faiths and of no faith. I was able to connect with people of other religions and of no religion and enjoy engaging conversations on a whole raft of social issues. The same applied to subcultures and age categories. Young people in their teens and early 20's found it easy to communicate with me as well. We talked for hours about all the issues that were important to them. Particularly the hip hop generation who had been raised on MTV. For some strange reason, I understood them and the psychological drivers that fuelled their aspirations.

Before long, I became super connected with people on all levels of the socio-economic scale. From gangsters in the hood to politicians in parliament. Entrepreneurs and social activists all found common ground with me. I never really understood what it was they loved about being in my company but I had a deep sense that this is exactly where Jesus would be.

CONNECTING WITH YOUR COMMUNITY

Something profound happens to a minister when he or she connects with the community to which they are called. First of all, the condescending and judgemental attitudes disappear. Up until this time I had a simple text book explanation for human behaviour. People did deviant things because they were sinners or because they were possessed. It was easy to blame sin and the devil for crime, injustice, promiscuity, drug addictions and the like.

The problem with this simplistic and archaic world view is that it informs your response to human behaviour. Back then, we thought that the cure of all social ills was preaching the gospel and praying against the spiritual principalities that were orchestrating chaos on a cosmic level. We prayed, we fasted and we preached because that was the answer. However, it is easy to reach these simplistic conclusions from behind the fence. Once you get over the fence and actually connect with ordinary people you will start to discover some of the other drivers behind human behaviour.

SIGN POSTS

Most people do things that they personally disapprove of for two main reasons. Firstly because they don't think they have a choice. In this respect, your decisions in life are limited to the choices that you think are available to you at the time. In this case, a person's behaviour can be changed by a simple presentation of alternatives and options. No need to cast out the devil here; just present a realistic alternative. For example, many people in the hood (low income, government housing projects) believe that the only way out of the misery of urban poverty is crime. So they engage in it. Others believe that music is a way out or sport or religion. The truth is that the pathways out of poverty should be clearly signposted before the devil gets credit for high crime in low income communities.

Bind the devil and cast out the ruling spirits in a thousand prayer meetings but until you can sign post the route out of poverty and deprivation, you will experience high crime in low income communities. The facts speak for themselves and are the same in every country where income disparity creates a criminal class. If you doubt this simple idea, then please explain why it is that some of the most prayerful countries in the world seem to be cursed with a raft of social ills including poverty, crime, vice and political corruption?

EMOTIONAL PAIN

The second reason why people do crazy things is because they are trying to medicate emotional pain. I can relate to this in a very real way. You see, when I was severely depressed, I was in a constant state of emotional pain. Any relief, if only for a moment made perfect sense, even if it was not practically possible. Until you understand chronic emotional and psychological pain, you will never understand human behaviour.

Back to my point; I lost my sense of judgement for people. I could not Judge them. I was no different. So I soon developed a reputation for being an inclusive preacher who wouldn't judge or reject anyone no matter what they did. I suppose it was true, because I did not close the door on anyone. I simply had grace for that space.

INCLUSIVE

With my reputation for unconditional love and an understanding of the human dilemma, I soon got approached by church folks who felt it safe to tell me about their struggles. They came from all over the country and from different parts of the world. From preachers' kids to deacons' wives. To my surprise, the church world was no different to the world in which it sat. Every issue, challenge and problem that the world faced was in fact present in proportionate numbers within the church. Contrary to popular opinion, the church was not a congregation of saints. Instead; when the mask was pulled off, the church was more like a hospital in which broken people were receiving medical treatment. Some were better off than others but all were sick. There really is no room to judge the guy in the next bed when you are in bed yourself.

The gospel of grace invites imperfect people into a perfect relationship with a perfect God. A changed life may be the result of that relationship but is never a requirement for it. Come as you are says the gospel of grace. Likewise, holiness is a work of the Spirit and not a work of the flesh. God is holy; human beings are only holy in as much as they reflect God's nature. In other words God is the sun and we are the moon. He is holy, but we are only holy in as much as we reflect him. True holiness then, is the reflection of God in a human being. The question is not the length of your skirt or the knot of your tie, but, can I see God in you? That's holiness. It is a work of the Spirit for which man cannot take the credit. A man cannot take the credit for his changed life any more than the moon can claim to be a light source. It is not a source it is only a reflection.

Based on these two facts; the gospel of grace and the nature of true holiness, I advised people, when they approached me with self-destructive feelings of self hate, as follows:

God loves you completely and unconditionally. He welcomes you into a full relationship with himself whether you get the victory or not. A change may be the result of this relationship, but it is not a requirement for it. If God wants you to change, He'll change you in his own way and in his own time. For now, you should accept yourself, love yourself and get on with the business of living.

YOUR SPACE

Some people reading this chapter are feeling sick right now. Sick because you cannot imagine how a preacher of the gospel could connect with Muslims, atheists, gangsters, gays, business people and politicians while feeling totally comfortable in their company. Has he lost his mind? Possibly, but I found my heart and with it my gift, my grace, my space and my anointing.

None of us are called to occupy the same space. Your unique gifts and callings will place you in a unique sociological space for the purposes of ministry. Your assignment is to a people who are in a place; be it geographical, economic, social, psychological, emotional or spiritual place. You are called to a people in a place and you will have uncommon grace for that space.

> ***You are called to a people in a place and you will have uncommon grace for that space.***

Consider the Apostle Paul, who was the Apostle to the Gentiles. Strangely he was a Jewish Apostle to the Gentiles. And not just any Jew; a Pharisee of the Pharisees. A strictly religious and devoted adherent to the laws of Moses. God called him to be the chief messenger to the Gentile world. How did you stomach it Paul? How did you sit around tables full of pork and other unclean meats. How did you cope with Gentile culture or the lack thereof? The answer is simple; Paul had grace for his space. Not even Peter the primary Apostle, could stand in the shoes of Paul. He simply couldn't handle the Gentile environment because it was not his unique space.

Since my revelation of the Kingdom and of the invasion of world systems, I have worked with business people, political advocates, entertainers, journalist, community activists and more, who are tired of being a big fish in a small bowl and have instead opted to jump into the ocean and swim with the sharks. They are in industries and institutions that are rife with corruption, sleaze and overt promiscuity. They work daily alongside commercial animals who have no principles, scruples or morals and would sell their grandmother for a McDonalds' burger. They are hit on daily by sexual predators and are surrounded by a casual use of the 'F' word alongside blasphemous references to Christ.

Yet they provide a first class service, with a first class attitude and with first class results. How? By the uncommon grace they have for that space. I wouldn't last a day in certain fields and neither would you. But they have survived and thrived in it for years. I celebrate them. I applaud them and admire the courage and conviction of anyone who seeks to serve God in the kingdoms of men.

Can you imagine what it must have been like for Daniel, working in the royal courts of Babylon alongside fellow magicians, soothsayers and wizards. Most couldn't stomach it but Daniel had so much grace for that space and so much love for his fellows that he intervened to prevent Nebuchadnezzar from beheading them all.

Can you love people who are different? Can you respect another point of view? Can you agree to differ yet provide a first class service with the utmost care and consideration? Can you reserve judgement until all the facts are in place? Can you refuse to impose your rules on others who don't have your relationship with God? That's exactly what it takes to serve God in the Kingdoms of men.

CHAPTER 8
A LIFE LINE

One of the life-lines thrown out to me when I was in the thick of the storm came when I discovered self-development. After much prayer about the various circumstances I was facing, it felt as though God said to me; if you can't change the weather you can change your clothes. I knew what this meant. It meant that if I couldn't change my circumstances, then I should go to work on changing myself. It also meant that things were not going to change but I could change me. They were not going to get easier but I could get stronger. The suggestion was that I could personally out grow my situation and it was only too much to bear because my mental and social muscles weren't yet strong enough to carry the load.

I was exhausted and burned out from trying to work on 'it' and trying to change 'things'. But it seemed as though God wanted me to stop working on it or things and instead go to work on myself. This simple change of strategy brought with it a breath of fresh air because many of my frustrations started to leave when I stopped struggling to change the things that I could not. Instead, I was trying to change the one thing that I really could change and that was me.

I started by identifying 12 skills that, if mastered, would give me a strategic advantage in life. At the time, business never crossed my mind. I simply wanted to become more skillful on a personal and professional level. I had no clue that these skills would later define me as an a entrepreneur and give birth to a global enterprise. These skills included things like time management, stress management, emotional intelligence and NLP (Neuro-Linguistic Programming). Financial management, leadership, life-mapping, thought control and relationship strategies were then added to the mix. Self-development, speed learning techniques and of course some additional theology then concluded my list.

I began to relish the idea that I could outgrow my circumstances or in some psychological way; become bigger than the mountain in front of me.

I figured that with an advanced knowledge of these subjects and the acquisition of their corresponding skill sets, I would better be able to handle the inevitable surprises that life throws at us all. Perhaps I wouldn't buckle so easily or would be able to resolve matters more swiftly. I began to relish the idea that I could outgrow my circumstances or in some psychological way; become bigger than the mountain in front of me.

That year, I opened an account with Amazon and went crazy. In fact; Borders, Amazon, Barnes & Noble, when I was in the states, and WH Smiths were like candy stores to a kid. I was the kid in the candy store buying, collecting, reading and re-reading until the principles made sense. Travel time became learning time as I proceeded to assemble a huge library of audio books and learning programmes. These would end up on my iPod or in the car as I enrolled in the mobile university. Always wearing head phones or listening to audios in the car. I had become a learning addict and knowledge was my new drug.

I can't fully explain the rush, but for some reason I could not wait to get back to my books. My books were the last thing at night and the first thing in the morning. They were in the toilet, the bathroom, the living room and the bed room. After all, I was on my own, trying to come to terms with the demise of my ministry, the collapse of my marriage and the subsequent depression. It was as though the books were a life line from God.

I initially decided to give one month to each subject. It would be my year of personal growth and transformation. So I had 12 subjects and 12 months. The plan was to read five books on each subject each month and to attend as many short courses or seminars on any of the subjects at hand.

Because there was so much to read, listen to, watch and attend, I decided to start with speed learning techniques. I had become aware of some new thought around the science of learning and decided to master the subject. I bought several books and just as many audio programmes on speed reading, mind mapping, advanced memorisation techniques and other learning strategies. Truth be told I loved this subject so much that I never stopped peaking into those books even when I was on the other subjects.

Needless to say, the speed learning material turned me into a book python. I wasn't a book worm; I was literally swallowing them whole. This went on for the best part of two years and would see me devour 2 to 3 books per week. There were even times when I would read through a book in a day or two. I ended up going through 140 books in the first year and simply kept going the second year. I didn't pay too much attention to the person I was becoming because I was too engrossed in the subjects. But as you can guess; with all that knowledge in my head, I was changing in a very fundamental way.

WORD THOUGHTS

Reading has a profound effect on the reader because it is a medium for transmitting thoughts. Words are thoughts expressed in print or sound. Each word represents a thought and each sequence of words a sequence of thoughts. Because words are thoughts then new words create new thoughts. These new thoughts mix with your old thoughts to create a certain mental chemistry. New words enable you to think through a more complex sequence of thoughts. As a result, your creative and problem solving skills take a quantum leap into the realm of the extraordinary.

Because I read lots of thoughts, I was becoming a deep and creative thinker. In addition to becoming a deep thinker, I was becoming a more profound speaker and author. My vocabulary had expanded and my thinking had evolved. Whether it was a sermon or a seminar I was simply full of content and people began to notice. The speaking invitations began to pour in and the reviews were amazing.

Mind blowing, phenomenal and truly gifted, were among the words people used to describe the emerging Wayne Malcolm. Although I had no huge mega church, I became sought after by huge ministries, secular groups, government agencies and sales based organisations based solely on my unique content and delivery. To my pleasant surprise they were willing to pay top dollars for having me on the bill too.

ICAN THE BUSINESS

One of the outcomes of the year of investigation was a strong recommendation that I separate Wayne Malcolm Ministries from the local church. Up until that time we shared the office space and the two teams worked seamlessly as one. The difference was that Wayne Malcolm ministries managed my itinerate speaking engagements and my intellectual property. Up until the property crash in 2003, the local church absolutely adored my profile as an international conference speaker and never saw any difference between the two entities besides a few semantics. It was under this banner and with this team that I conducted crusades and conferences in India, South Africa, America and the Caribbean. No one saw a difference between the church and the itinerate ministry until the strong recommendations to split the two entities occurred.

To facilitate that split; I rebranded Wayne Malcolm Ministries as iCAN. It stands for the international coaching achievers network. We rented some office space with training rooms and took a small staff to work. The vision was clear; our organisation would provide coaching, training and seminar services to people who were serious about self-development and personal growth. My main aim was to throw out to others the lifeline that God had thrown out to me. I wanted to teach them in seminar style the art of living by design; living deliberately, intentionally, passionately and on purpose. I would teach them to set goals, to draw up a life map, to manage their time and resources and above all, to live their dreams.

I had already rebranded my annual conference, which was originally called WAR, to Live The Dream and used it to teach a range of life management strategies. We would focus on repairing self esteem, creating a compelling vision for the future and implementing a plan of action. When speaking in churches; I would challenge them to grow their skill base. 'Your dream is not too big', I would holla, 'but you might be too small.'

I went one step further and tried to make iCAN totally inclusive by dropping all religious references and welcoming people of all faiths or no faith to join the programme. I still remember how difficult it was to teach for an hour without saying praise the Lord, amen, hallelujah. You see, up until that point I had never done it. But I soon learned how to speak or teach whilst creating a safe space for others.

THE CHURCH HAD QUESTIONS

Some of the church people really struggled with my new emphasis on invading the power bases of society, self-development and living your dreams. It wasn't churchy enough and conflicted with their personal theology. Rumours were flying everywhere; 'He's leaving...if his iCAN takes off'; 'He's not coming back.' I was not aware of all the rumours at the time, but I did know that there was a tension between a section of my local church and the whole idea of an iCAN. As a result of the tension many of my members never attended a course or an event that was branded iCAN. It was Bishop's thing, Bishop's business or Bishop's escape. Unfortunately, splitting the ministry was bad news for all because it meant that I now had two offices, two staff, two responsibilities and none of them got the best of me.

WIDER QUESTIONS

I remember teaching a leadership seminar at a famous Bible college when one of the attendees asked a question. He said, 'The S word of Christianity is suffering not success, don't you agree?' I said, 'No I don't agree because success is the point of suffering. Pointless suffering doesn't glorify God. Jesus suffered in order to succeed in his mission to redeem the world. He didn't just suffer for the sake of it'. I finally said that, 'If we confuse the end with the means, then we will make the means an end in itself'.

I am not sure that my brother was prepared for such a philosophical answer. He just went quiet and the class continued. However his little voice spoke for thousands if not millions of Christians who had become disillusioned with the current brand of prosperity teaching. Many wondered if I was not simply teaching prosperity along with many of the charlatans who had recently been exposed in the main stream media. They seemed to doubt that God was in anyway concerned with their quality of life. He simply wanted them saved and holy so He could take them to heaven. He didn't want them healthy and happy and certainly frowned on material wealth. I noticed that there was a deep rooted suspicion of any teaching that emphasised success, prosperity or happiness on this side of eternity.

The resistance was baffling at first so I decided to do what I loved and to research the problem more thoroughly. I found out that the Christian community was fundamentally split between the Kingdom then and the Kingdom now advocates. Of course the Bible teaches a Kingdom then and now. The Kingdom is here right now and will be even more glorious in the future. The 'Kingdom then' advocates said that we will all be happy, healthy and wealthy in the sweet bye and bye, when we all get to heaven. The 'Kingdom now' advocates said, we won't need it in heaven; we need it now! I decided to study it from another point of view.

I studied this issue using Abraham Maslow's hierarchy of need. Abraham Maslow was a behavioural psychologist in the 70's who developed an interesting theory about human behaviour. He claimed that people were motivated to meet their needs on five distinct levels. First were the primary physiological needs for food, water and shelter from the elements. Then came the need for safety or security. Next was the need to love and belong. The last two had to do with esteem and self-actualising. Maslow argues that secondary needs only become important once primary needs are met. This means that if people are deprived of food, water, shelter and security, they will not be interested in love, belonging, esteem or self-actualisation.

I applied this theory to many of the critics of my message and discovered that the most critical were the well to do middle classes who had job security, home ownership and a life insurance policy. Those who favoured my message were the poor and marginalised victims of social injustice and economic disparity.

SOCIAL JUSTICE

My own social consciousness started way back in the BC of my life when I was a Rastafarian. Music was the main medium of learning for me back then and the music was very political in nature. We were reminded that black Africans were enslaved by Europeans and used as a cheap workforce to create wealth for the white ruling class. We were reminded of the struggle for basic human rights and then for basic civil rights. We knew about segregation, Jim Crow and apartheid. We were proud of our ancestors, proud of our progress and proud of our culture. At the same time we had no respect for parliament, the monarchy, the church of England, the Police, the judiciary or any other aspect of the British establishment, because they were all seen as instruments of oppression. They served to sustain our status as a second class minority who needed to be managed, marginalised and otherwise controlled.

Racism, on an institutional level, was a fact of life for young blacks in the 70's and 80's and Rastafarianism seemed to explain why. The problem with the Rastafarian position was that it tended to generate a form of reverse racism and a desire for vengeance. I'm not sure this was deliberate, but this was the effect it had on us as kids. We wanted to hurt the establishment, embarrass it and otherwise remind it that we were still here. The philosophy presented few if any solutions to the problems of racism but it did raise our level of social consciousness.

When I became a Christian, these matters slowly slipped off the radar and were instead replaced by evangelism and the propagation of the gospel. It was more important that people got saved than it was for them to have equal access to public services and a level economic playing field. After all; housing, education, health care and employment are hardly the issue when a soul is suspended between heaven and hell. This is why Karl Marx called Christianity 'the opiate of the masses'. It was a drug that made people passive, compliant and cooperative with the very people who were exploiting them. He observed that the Orthodox church had become a tool in the hands of the aristocracy. It was their job to convince the masses to exchange the 'here and now' for the 'there and then'. The church did this so well that Marx called it a drug.

After my grace awaking and subsequent theological transition, I realised that I too was on the drug. I had become an instrument of oppression by simply preaching the theology of the well to do middle classes. I did not have good news for the poor, neither did I have a plan for ending poverty. I didn't even have a Biblical frame work for social action and felt like I was failing my generation. The majority of blacks still lived in substandard housing, still had the highest exclusion rates from school, still had the highest incarceration rates of any ethnic group and still were being disproportionately stopped, searched and arrested. Black boys were disproportionally dying in police custody or being committed to mental health institutions and the life expectancy of a black male was considerably lower than that of his white counterparts.

My community was mad. I mean really angry. Not just at society but also at the church for standing by and doing nothing. Of course the church at large was doing something but it always felt like too little too late. I sat in many cross denominational church leadership forums in which social issues were discussed. However, for many, that's where it stopped while the rest struggled to determine, let alone deliver a response.

Because of my understanding of the role that particular brands of Christianity played in perpetuating slavery, segregation and apartheid, I became suspicious of any Christian group that made light of social justice and economic opportunity. I felt that they had abandoned the poor and were now kissing up to the rich and powerful. Of course, social justice and economic opportunity became a centre piece of my message and work.

THE ACTIVIST

With a renewed social conscience and an outstanding speaking gift, I set about networking with existing social activists. I would attend community meetings and rallies. I would speak up at community forums, give press interviews, challenge the authorities, write articles, and hold the hands of families who lost members in police custody. At times, I was the only preacher in the room and to my surprise they would typically ask me to open the proceedings with prayer and then to deliver a message. I met with the Reverend Jesse Jackson and started plugging into a raft of other civil rights campaigners.

My voice and tone during these times changed considerably. I too was angry at the blatant injustice and lack of genuine opportunity for the working classes and ethnic minorities. The more you get into the world of the activists, the more injustice you become aware of. I was appalled at the statistics but at the same time, I had serious concerns about the strategies employed by the majority of social action groups.

My concerns came from my own political philosophy. You see, I lean to the right in that I believe in a small government, civil liberty and free markets. At the same time, I lean to left when it comes to helping the poor. I majored in sociology at school and understood the philosophical divide between left and right. My heart was to the left, but my head was to the right and I guess that left me somewhere in the middle. My problem was that most of the social activism was coming from the far left and carried with it a whole raft of other issues for which I had no real interest. It wasn't possible to simply defend the poor; you also had to defend the whole spectrum of left wing ideology.

I began to scrutinise the methods and messages coming out of various social action groups. I also looked at their track record for getting results in an attempt to develop my own strategic approach to social problems. One that would sit well with my new theology and political philosophy. Well, I found it and when I did; iCAN began to change direction.

POLITICAL LITERACY

Many of my social activist friends insisted on pursuing the old civil rights style strategy for addressing the issues of social justice and economic fairness. Put simply; the strategy involved putting pressure on or embarrassing the State into releasing more funds and changing legislation. You simply leveraged the media as a tool for embarrassing or pressurising the State. Hence any opportunity to get in front of the cameras or to make the front pages were seized with rigour. Of course, this approach has delivered unquestionable results and was the guiding philosophy behind the civil rights movement. It was responsible for the collapse of apartheid in South Africa. However it relied on two things which were missing from the UK experience, namely; political literacy and political consensus.

Democracy is a numbers game; plain and simple. In order to apply the pressure, you needed to be able to mobilise people in large numbers on a big scale. In the black community we were typically unsuccessful at mobilising large numbers to make a political point. This was partly because the black community had lost its homogenous identity and was now quite fragmented. We now sat on different sides of the political divide and had very few issues about which we all felt the same. This wasn't the case for Martin Luther King. Segregation affected all African Americans and therefore his voice resonated with the masses even if many disagreed with his approach. In the UK there are very few issues about which we all feel passionate and even less consensus on what to do about them.

It was also because the black majority church, which already entertains hundreds of thousands of black Brits, is only just waking up its social responsibility and its colossal power to hold government to account. So with a fragmented black community and an undecided church, the efforts of the activists were ending in frustration. The politicians knew it too and were not terribly worried about the black vote because they knew that we probably would not generate the numbers needed to make a difference.

I quickly concluded that the answer lay in education. 'Democracy without political literacy is a fantasy'; I would thunder from podiums in public meetings and rallies. I realised that our people were not politically educated and didn't really understand how our democracy works. We felt disenfranchised and left the politics to someone else. We did not understand the nature of the beast called government and had no idea where to apply the pressure. I became an advocate for political literacy and decided that politics would appear in the iCAN curriculum.

ECONOMIC STRENGTH

Most of our political efforts were frustrated by a lack of funds. This became my main bone of contention with the activists. They seemed obsessed with getting more money from the government. They literally wanted the government or its agencies to fund their activities. It was as though money was the end game and the answer to all social ills. If it doesn't work; throw money at it. This was their ultimate answer to youth crime, unemployment, housing, education, health care and any other public service. If it doesn't work; throw money at it.

My first problem was with public funds. In my experience the government only ever fund its own objectives. Qualifying for funding typically means; bending your proposition until it meets the criteria set out by the government. That criteria typically excludes grass roots groups who are in a position to make a real difference. For example, many churches seeking to provide services to vulnerable people did not qualify for funding because they didn't meet the equalities criteria. They would have to drop any references to faith and come in line with government objectives in order to receive funding. This was not just happening to churches, but to a whole raft of grass roots organisations who are forced to bend and twist their proposition until it ticks all the boxes.

My second problem was with the co-dependency on government agencies that their approach generated. Many of our businesses were co-dependent as was our voluntary sector. So much in the black community relied on government funds that it became embarrassing. To cap it all we felt we were entitled to it.

Other ethnic minorities took another approach. They focused on building their own economies through enterprise. Two or more families would huddle together in one flat to keep their costs low. They would then invest their money into a little business like a post office or a corner shop. Before long they owned the strip and each family moved into their own accommodation. They also focused on education, insisting that their children did well at school and that they studied a profession. They were grooming doctors, lawyers, accountants and dentists who would eventually set up their own practise and employ their own people. They banded together to purchase fast food franchises and otherwise began moving steadily up the social and economic scale. Today, many of their children drive prestige cars and are living the dream.

These groups all had a strong family and work ethic. Family for them was not just a nuclear unit, but included the extended family of grandparents, aunts, uncles and cousins. This is something we were losing in our own community. Children obeyed their parents and couples were supported by a wider social network. Religion also played a role in the creation of these cultural economies, because it constituted an extended family and preserved their cultural identity.

In light of these observations, we had become our own worse enemy. The welfare system and entitlement thinking had decimated our own work ethic and the family as a social unit was fading away. We had more single mothers and absent fathers than any other group. You simply can't throw money at that. These problems were more complex than money could solve. I do not say these things from the moral high ground. This was not a preacher condescending on society. My own marriage had ended and I never felt qualified to champion the family message. I deeply believe in marriage and think that a marital breakdown is tragic. But where I was so embarrassed about my own situation, I never felt qualified to lead on that issue. But that does not mean I couldn't see how important family was to God, to society and to the economic growth of a people. Many of these ideas guided my own approach to parenting and as a result, my boys still think I'm the best dad in the world. I sincerely wish I could have been a better role model for them, but sometimes leadership is about managing difficult realities and making the best out of a bad situation. The best I could make out of my failed marriage was to be the best dad that I could be.

HANDWRITING ON THE WALL

I began to see the handwriting on the wall for the state-dependent masses, when the credit crunch hit us in 2008 and governments around the world proceeded to bail out banks and big corporations to the tune of trillions. My limited knowledge of economics said; 'We'll pay for this'. I knew that taxes would go up and public services would get thinner no matter which government came to power. I had enough political knowledge to know that the crisis was beyond party politics and that the next government would be forced to make cuts. I also knew that the cuts would hit the public sector hard and would result in many losing their jobs.

It was also clear that the private sector would sustain huge losses because of its reliance on credit. The storm brewing in the horizon was a deep and long recession in which the poor would get poorer and the rich would get richer. There is a difference between poverty and economic disparity. Poverty means that there is not enough. But disparity occurs when a minority have more than enough while the majority have not enough. It is the income and lifestyle gap between the poorest and the richest living in the same space.

I knew that mass unemployment would spark an increase in a number of other social ills including drug abuse, mental illness, marital breakdowns and crime. All the things our community was already struggling with were about to get worse. I knew that our voluntary sector would be diminished if not completely destroyed and that anything dependent on government funding would sustain monumental losses.

ENTERPRISE TRAINING

That's when iCAN took a decisive turn and began focusing almost exclusively on enterprise training. Nothing short of an entrepreneurial awaking would save us from the days ahead. We had to entrepreneurialise our community or watch more of our kids go to prison. I realised that jobs would get fewer and farther apart and that the future looked horrible for job-dependent people. At the same time, I knew that recessions always come loaded with enterprise opportunities for those in the know. Self employment was the only realistic response to mass unemployment and I was determined to show our students how.

Unsurprisingly, my new emphasis on entrepreneurship and enterprise training was met with scepticism by churchy people who didn't understand the kingdom. They simply watched while I ranted on about a seminar, a course or a book I had written. Likewise many in our community silently felt it was just a money making scheme. Such is the plight of a prophet. You see, prophets were originally called seers because they saw things that others could not see. They had foresight unlike critics who only have hindsight. A true prophet is someone who has the courage to say what he sees. It takes courage because at first, no one else can see it and you sound like a lunatic. However, eventually, everyone sees what the prophet saw.

The same proved true of my campaign to entrepreneurialise the community. Eventually people caught on. How could they not? Our whole society is now awake to the fact that enterprise training must be put in schools and that self employment skills may make the difference between total state-dependence and a better quality of life.

I started to get invitations from mega and para-church organisations who then dubbed me the Business Bishop and the Entrepreneur's Pastor. They wanted me to do business seminars and to share the new rules for making and keeping money in the wake of a global recession. I took these seminars around the United Kingdom and to various parts of the United States and I am currently making preparations to bring our unique brand of enterprise training to the four corners of the earth.

CHAPTER 9

THE BUTTERFLY SECRET

Now I'm going to let you in on a secret. It is a principle for which there are thousands of patterns in nature, the people around you and the Bible itself. It is the secret to fulfilling your destiny. The beautiful thing about a universal principle is that the patterns are universal also. Once you discover the principle, the patterns just start appearing everywhere until the principle becomes obvious and utterly undeniable.

Throughout my life you will notice a thread or a theme. You will note that same theme running through the lives of many others whose lives become extraordinary or who are clearly destined for greatness. For some reading this book, my life is the story of confusion. In their minds the subtitle should read; A journey from nuts to insane! He starts off deluded and ends up even more so! Why does his life even matter? Who really wants to know? Please note these words because they describe the language patterns of someone who is still a caterpillar.

A caterpillar cannot fly because it has not yet experienced the metamorphosis that would give it wings.

However, many others will notice a man on a journey, following a light which at times appears and at others disappears. This light takes him to the tops of mountains and to the belly of valleys but is always there. The light could otherwise be called; conviction or revelation so that whenever my understanding changed, I changed and moved in the direction of that light. Following your inner light requires deep conviction and true courage because it will often take you from a place of comfort and security to one of discomfort and uncertainty. But even though your understanding will take you to some dark places, following it is non-negotiable. If you survive the journey you will begin to understand why the light takes you through highs and lows and why the dark places were absolutely critical to your own success.

DREAM VERSUS DESTINY

We all have dreams in life, but your dreams are not your destiny. They are simply the bait that God uses to draw you along a path. Your dreams are the small picture that you see, but your destiny is the big picture that God sees. Nelson Mandela had the dream of a free and fair South Africa in which a true democracy would give every man an equal say. He dreamed of an end to apartheid and gave his life for his dream. His destiny as the president of a free South Africa never crossed his mind. But it was the pursuit of his dreams that moulded him into the person that would fulfil his greater destiny.

Your destiny is the ultimate and final contribution that your life makes to the progress of humanity. The truth is that you don't know your destiny and will not know it until you chase your dreams. In the Bible, Joseph was the dreamer who became the prince of Egypt. All he had was a dream; a small piece in the puzzle that would become his destiny. It's as though God lets you see pieces of the puzzle but never the big picture. The big picture only ever emerges as you go.

> 1 ***Now the LORD had said unto Abram,***
> ***Get thee out of thy country, and from thy***
> ***kindred, and from thy father's house, unto***
> ***a land that I will show thee:***
> 2 ***And I will make of thee a great nation, and***
> ***I will bless thee, and make thy name great;***
> ***and thou shalt be a blessing:***
> 3 ***And I will bless them that bless thee, and***
> ***curse him that curseth thee: and in thee shall***
> ***all families of the earth be blessed.***
>
> *Genesis* 12:1-3

Notice that Abraham was to go to a place that he would afterwards see. That is how destiny works; it only ever appears as you go.

As you chase your dreams you pass through a process known as METAMORPHOSIS, or transformation. You change because the journey is designed to change you. Of course you can quit at any time; abandoning your dreams and never becoming the person you could be. Or you can keep on going and experience the transformation that your destiny demands.

Keeping on requires high levels of motivation but let's not confuse motivation with inspiration. Inspiration is a burst of light (knowledge) that induces feelings of certainty about what is now possible for you. You may be inspired by someone else's story. Maybe my own story will inspire you. Whatever the case; inspiration is a feeling that doesn't always translate into a decision. Motivation on the other hand is..YOUR MOTIVE FOR TAKING ACTION! It is the motive or reason for your action. The word comes from a root word which means to move. It is a doing word that presupposes activity and then supplies a reason for that activity.

Many people say they are motivated when infact they are simply inspired. They feel motivated but the truth is that you are only motivated if you actually move. The people who follow their dreams in life are highly motivated. Something is moving them to act. There is a reason why they will not quit. It is as though they are running on a different sort of fuel to the rest of us. Why not just quit? Come on, throw in the towel. They are knocked down but never out. They seem to bounce back from a set back or break through right after a breakdown. What are these people on?

They have indeed discovered a fuel that keeps them going and glowing in the face of serious setbacks, disappointment and frustration. The primary motivator is PAIN. We are all motivated by the pain/pleasure principle. That is the need to avoid pain or to obtain pleasure. However, when it comes to the journey that transforms a you into the person who can fulfil destiny; PAIN is the primary motivator.

THE SECRET

The butterfly has a secret that only the people who have experienced metamorphosis can relate to. The butterfly is beautiful to look at. A masterful work of art and a miracle of nature. People typically avoid flies, swinging anything at them in an attempt to push them away. But not the butterfly. When one appears, we gaze with admiration. We try to get as close as possible because of the beauty, the grace and the elegance with which they dance on thin air. Not only is the butterfly beautiful to behold but it is also extremely powerful. It can be proved in physics that the flap of a butterflies wings on one side of the world can affect the weather in another part of the world.

Did you see the film called 'The butterfly effect'? It's about small incidental events having colossal consequences. That film is based on the science of the butterfly's power to altar the course of history and to effect massive change on a global scale. We already know from history that little people can make big things happen and that an individual life can change the lives of millions. This is true of Jesus Christ whose short stay in the flesh has changed the lives of millions for the last 2000 years. Nelson Mandela, Martin Luther King, Ghandi and others altered the course of human history and changed the lives of millions. Such is the nature of the beautiful butterfly; elegant and graceful, yet powerful beyond the imagination.

The butterfly has a secret. You see, it didn't start out as a butterfly; it started life as a caterpillar. Ugly, slow, undesirable and bound by gravity to cling onto branches and leaves. No wings, no real colour and no power. But it became a butterfly through a process. A caterpillar moults and sheds its skin several times before the real metamorphosis begins. That's like many people who go about reinventing themselves and otherwise making over the old person. But there comes a time when the caterpillar begins to spin a silky web so tight that it forms a hard shell around its self. It literally proceeds to bury itself in the critical darkness that would permit the process of transformation.

CRITICAL DARKNESS

Real transformation happens in darkness and not light. It is the dark seasons of your life that produce the transformations necessary for you to manifest your true destiny. Let me start with a few Biblical examples and then bring it down to earth.

Jesus was transformed from a carpenter's son to the Son of God with power, after 40 days and 40 nights alone with the devil. The wilderness was the cocoon that would transform the caterpillar into a butterfly. He then made another transition from a miracle worker in Israel to the Saviour of the world, but only through the cross and a tomb. The process by which Jesus became the Saviour of the world was the process of death, burial and resurrection. His death and burial provided the tomb in which his butterfly could be formed.

Joseph was transformed from a slave in Potiphars house to a prince in Egypt but only after a period of imprisonment. Moses became Israel's deliverer but only after a period of exile in which he lived as a fugitive. Please note; Moses started life as a prince in Egypt but lost it all before he would become a deliverer.

Samson delivered Israel from the Philistines but only after he was bound, blinded and subject to public ridicule. Daniel became a prince in Persia, but only after he endured the cocoon of the Lions' den. Good things come from many places, but God things always come out of a cocoon in the form of a wilderness, a fiery trial or a barren womb. The examples are endless but they all teach the same principle.

Do not despise the dark days of your life nor the dark side of your personality. For these are the very things that destiny uses to position you for greatness. These are the very forces that mould you into another shape. Once inside the cocoon, a caterpillar proceeds to eat itself until its organs become liquid. The liquid then sets in the mould print inside the cocoon. The organs reassemble themselves in another order and wings are formed. The pressure then squeezes more fluid into its wings until they are fully formed. The last stage is eating and fighting its way out of the cocoon.

Don't despise the dark days of your life nor the dark side of your personality. For these are the very things that destiny uses to position you for greatness.

Any attempt to interfere with this process will prevent the full formation of the new creature inside. It must be left in darkness until the metamorphosis occurs. Once it has taken place, the shell cannot hold it. It bursts out with power and grace. The same is true of all genuinely great people. Their greatness is formed in the darkness but manifested in the light. Often when we see great people doing great things, we think of them as lucky or fortunate. We often do not see the darkness in which their greatness was formed. But mark my words well, greatness is formed in darkness before it appears in light.

YOUR DARK SIDE

You should give yourself the same gift that God gave you, namely; unconditional love. People who accept and respect themselves, warts an all, are less prone to depression, chronic stress, personality disorders and mental illness. They are more likely to survive the inevitable storms that life brings their way. The truth is that God uses both your strengths and weaknesses in order to carry out his plan. This is why God doesn't take your weaknesses away, He simply uses them to reposition you in life. They play a part and have a place in your destiny.

For example, many believe that Samson was a strong man with a weakness for women. They think he should have had the wisdom and strength to resist their advances or that he would have been better off without that weakness. However, the Bible says this:

> ***And Samson went down to Timnath, and saw a woman in Timnath of the daughters of the Philistines. 2] And he came up, and told his father and his mother, and said, I have seen a woman in Timnath of the daughters of the Philistines: now therefore get her for me to wife. 3] Then his father and his mother said unto him, Is there never a woman among***

> ***the daughters of thy brethren, or among all my people, that thou goest to take a wife of the uncircumcised Philistines? And Samson said unto his father, Get her for me; for she pleaseth me well. 4] But his father and his mother knew not that it was of the LORD, that he sought an occasion against the Philistines: for at that time the Philistines had dominion over Israel.***
>
> *Judges 14:1-4*

Samson's affection for strange women was actually a gift from God for the purpose of leading him towards his destiny. What if he took his fathers advice and called off the relationship? What if he only had eyes for the 'saved women'? what if he never fell for Delilah? His destiny required both weakness and strength. So does everyone's destiny. Don't despise your weaknesses or your dark side because your destiny requires them of you.

The Butterfly's secret is this: My pain produced my power, it is the source of my power and the maker of my shape. In order to transform; a caterpillar must literally eat and digest itself until its organs are fluid. That fluid can then be moulded into a new shape. This metaphor is striking. It suggests that pain can be converted into power if digested. Pain can become fuel for your future if you digest it.

The future belongs to the butterflies. Those who can convert emotional pain into spiritual fuel. Those who allow the dark episodes of their life to create a better person and not a bitter one.

THE OBVIOUS CONNECTION

A dear friend of mine once told me that greatness is reserved for those who make the obvious connection. I didn't know what he was talking about until I was recently in a cocoon. In that cocoon I suddenly saw the obvious connection. Namely the connection between my life and my work. You see, up until this point, I have kept my personal life a mystery. No body really knew me because I came from a school of thought which said, 'Don't give your enemies any ammunition. Don't show any weaknesses or they'll get you'. I realised in that dark place actually, the opposite was true. Transparency and vulnerability does not empower your enemy, it disempowers them. I realise that there is an obvious connection between my life and my message.

I am no stranger to struggle, disappointment, set backs or frustration. The episodes listed in this book are only a few of the many that have moulded and shaped my character for a greater destiny. But I unknowingly converted those things into fuel. That is the butterfly's secret.

Singers and artists who make this connection, create classic works of art that survive the test of time. This is because their soul is in their work. When you sing from the pain or joy of a personal experience, the song takes on a new form. It connects to the soul of others and is immortalised through consensus.

CHAPTER 10

BITTER OR BETTER

Bitterness is a root sin in that it sprouts many branches and yields a poisonous fruit. The fruits of bitterness include: anger, resentment, revenge, hate, spite and jealousy. Unfortunately, people who walk through life harbouring these emotions are literally incapable of discovering, let alone manifesting their true destiny. Bitterness warps your perception of reality; it clouds your judgments and drains you of critical creative energy. I'm sure you have met people who seemed to carry a chip on their shoulder. They are angry with someone, with society and with God himself. They are typically suspicious of everyone and everything. They put up social barriers making it impossible to truly connect with them on a deeper level.

Worse of all, a bitter person feels justified in dishing out pain to others. It's as though they want the world to feel their pain! They find it easy to criticize, undermine, disregard and otherwise belittle the achievements of others. Spiteful words flow freely from their mouth while they relish any gossip or rumours that drag down their perceived offender.

Bitterness is a root sin because it is ultimately a sin against God himself. Let me explain; the bitter person is ultimately angry with God. This anger is usually masked by anger at other people who they believe played a part in some painful incident. However, underneath their anger with others is the haunting knowledge that God let it happen. In this respect, God is ultimately to blame for the incidents, episodes and circumstances that caused the emotional pain.

As a counsellor, I have observed adults in their 40's who carried bitterness and hatred for one or both parents. They were abused, abandoned or neglected by one or both and cannot get over it. Even after their parents have gone these individuals still seek justice or retribution for the episodes that came to define them. They literally place the blame for every other disappointment in life at the feet of their parents. The reason why they cannot hold down a relationship or a job, goes right back to the abuse or neglect of someone in their past. They are playing the blame game with life. The problem is that if you win the blame game; you lose the life game.

I have personally been the subject of the bitterness of others and the object of their wrath. This first occurred after I shed the skin of legalism to embrace the gospel of grace. Of course many rejoiced at the new found liberty that would characterize our ministry, but others looked back on the legalistic years and concluded that a huge portion of their life had been stolen by me. They figured that I lead them into a life of strict separation from the world and that they perhaps missed opportunities that may have occurred if we had never met. They blamed me for their inability to find a partner in life; citing the time lost, the psychological damage and the missed opportunities.

In fact, the same phenomenon occurred every time I shed my theological and philosophical skin. When I moved from evacuation to invasion, there were a few who felt that the evacuation doctrines prevented them from pursuing higher education and a proper career path. They had now lost the time. Their career failures were my fault. The same occurred when I discovered the kingdom and began to engage in business, politics and the media. A small minority couldn't handle it and began to regret ever meeting me. They would move on to other ministries and would make it their life's mission to convince everyone else to do the same. At one stage I saw ex-members outside of our church, handing out tracts and flyers inviting them to another ministry.

MAN WORSHIP

The one thing that all of those people had in common was their search for the perfect leader who was absolutely in touch with God and lived an exemplary life. They wanted a God; not a man to lead them. This way they could abdicate any personal responsibility and place it all at his feet. These were professional blame-gamers who had successfully won the blame game but had lost the game of life. Paralyzed by bitterness and hate; they had learned all the wrong lessons from their God-ordained journey in life.

The truth is that your minister is not, cannot and must not be perfect. This is the clear teaching of the Bible:

> ***For every high priest taken from among men is ordained for men in things pertaining to God, that he may offer both gifts and sacrifices for sins: 2] Who can have compassion on the ignorant, and on them that are out of the way; for that he himself also is compassed with infirmity. 3] And by reason hereof he ought, as for the people, so also for himself, to offer for sins. 4] And no man taketh this honour unto himself, but he that is called of God, as was Aaron.***
>
> *Hebrews 5:1-4*

The Christian minister must be able to identify with the realities of the human condition. Without identification there can be no compassion. The word compassion means; 'common suffering', which is only possible for people who can relate to suffering. This is why God specifically chooses human beings to lead human beings. A careful reading of Scripture will show that every one of our faith heroes were flawed. In fact, this is one of the proofs of Inspiration. Those doubting the Divine inspiration of the Scriptures must explain why any writer would deliberately mar the reputation of his own heroes. Yet in our Bible; every patriarch, prophet and king is exposed as incomplete, imperfect and incapable of perfection. From Abraham to Moses, from David to the apostle Paul; everyone is marred, flawed and exposed. There is only one person who emerges from history without spot, wrinkle, blemish or any such thing. He is the spotless and sinless Son of God who took away the sins of the world.

The reason why the imperfections of spiritual leaders are so carefully and deliberately documented in Scripture, is so that none of us would be tempted to worship a spiritual leader no matter how charismatic their gifting or how magnetic their personality. Only God should be worshipped but his vessels should not. Imperfections do not disqualify a Spiritual leader, instead they qualify him or her to identify with and relate to the realities of the human condition.

The Christian church at large is struggling to come to terms with some high profile and public failures of its leaders. A number of mega church pastors, TV evangelists and Para-church leaders have all come under the spotlight as their marriages failed, their finances failed and their sexual orientations were exposed. This was and always is a big blow to the brand but it was an even bigger blow to those who idolized and venerated these ministers. Again, while some got bitter, many others have gotten better because their expectations of a leader are now more realistic.

My view is that many of these leaders would not have fallen so hard and so fast if the expectations of them were more realistic and if the culture of the church allowed for more ministerial transparency. When my marriage failed; we both agreed a no ask, no tell policy. We had already committed to being there for our boys and so divorce was not even on the table. We would simply live apart, raise our children and only tell if asked. It wasn't until our boys had grown up that we finally agreed the terms of a divorce. Of course our closest friends knew what was happening but our congregation at large were left to speculate. In hindsight this was a huge mistake because speculation quickly becomes allegation and before you know it, everyone has his or her own version of events.

My prediction is that the culture of the church will and must evolve to where ministerial transparency is celebrated as a mark of strength as opposed to a sign of weakness. I think that the church of the future will be less naïve, less gullible and less demanding of its leaders. Instead it will be more affirming, more forgiving and more tolerant of a minister who dares to lift the curtain and place his personal struggles on display.

INTEGRITY

Of course a spiritual leader should practice what they preach and otherwise demonstrate integrity. These are not conflicting ideas when you understand that it is possible to have integrity and yet be imperfect. The word integrity does not mean perfection; it means the integration of different parts into one whole. It is the quality of being one and the same from whatever angle. Even if aspects of your life are broken; transparency can integrate that brokenness into a marvellous whole. If you can successfully integrate your strengths and weaknesses into a fully functioning whole, then you in fact have integrity. One of the reasons that I wanted to quit the ministry was my understanding of this passage:

> ***This is a true saying, If a man desire the office of a bishop, he desireth a good work. 2] A bishop then must be blameless, the husband of one wife, vigilant, sober, of good behaviour, given to hospitality, apt to teach; 3] Not given***

to wine, no striker, not greedy of filthy lucre;
but patient, not a brawler, not covetous;
4] One that ruleth well his own house, hav-
ing his children in subjection with all gravity;
5] (For if a man know not how to rule his own
house, how shall he take care of the church of
God?) 6] Not a novice, lest being lifted up with
pride he fall into the condemnation of the dev-
il. 7] Moreover he must have a good report
of them which are without; lest he fall into
reproach and the snare of the devil.

1Timothy 3:1-7

This passage lists the qualifications of a Bishop and as far as I could see, I was no longer Biblically qualified to be one. At one stage I was providing a ministerial covering, mentorship and leadership to hundreds of churches world-wide. I even had a Bishop wanting to put 20,000 churches under my leadership. However, I ran away from these opportunities because I no longer felt qualified to lead.

The breakthrough came when I had a conversation with my boys. They were telling me about some of their friends at school whose parents had split up and in particular the embarrassing way in which they did it. They then thanked me for the way I handled my own situation with dignity and skill. I was shocked because I felt as though I had failed them, however they felt the opposite. They felt that I had managed a bad situation exceptionally well. They commended me on the fact that they had never seen me and their mother argue and that they never felt abandoned by any of us. They now had a great relationship with both mum and dad, and mum and dad were still best of friends. To them this was amazing and to my shock their own friends were saying the same thing. 'Your dad handled his business really well', they would say.

This was a relief, but the real relief came when I revisited the passage that caused me to run away from my Bishopric. Then it lept out at me; what qualifies a Bishop is not a perfect house, but the ability to manage what ever occurs in that house. 'Ruling well' meant managing well. It meant managing both opportunity and adversity. After that revelation I decided to focus on managing whatever life throws at me. This is a more realistic approach to life and ministry. You cannot change the weather but you can change your clothes. If it's too hot you wear less, if it's too cold, you wear more. This understanding shifted my locus of control.

After that revelation I decided to focus on managing whatever life throws at me.

In psychology, the locus of control refers to the seat of power. Those with an external locus believed that they were victims of circumstances over which they had no control. Whether it was the economy, society or the behaviour of others. They had no control and had to accept their circumstances as fate. But those whose locus of control was internal believed that they had the power to change things and that the future was in their hands. This simple shift in my understanding restored my sense of control. I now understood that my trials had not disqualified me but rather they had qualified me to lead. I also realized that these circumstances had not defined me but rather they had refined me in preparation for a greater destiny.

DESTINY

Your dreams are not your destiny and your destiny is not your dreams. Your dreams are simply the bait that God uses to pull or push you along a path. However your destiny is much, much bigger than your little dreams because destiny is the Divine purpose for which you were born. In this respect, your dream is a piece of the puzzle but your destiny is the big picture. The dream is what you see with your limited understanding, but your destiny is what God saw when He fired you into the world.

The value is in the path or the journey; not in the dream. That is why many of our dreams evaporate or disintegrate before we actually lay hold of them. You may spend years in pursuit of a dream only to find it disappear once all the hard work is done. This is because the dream was only ever bait that lured you along a path. The point was never the dream; it was always the path. The journey itself was designed to correct and perfect you for a greater destiny. It is your necessary preparation for power. Without the path, your destiny would destroy you or you would destroy it. That is why God didn't just simply pick up Hebrew slaves and drop them off in the Promised Land. It was the path that would prepare them for the promise.

When you understand that the value is in the path, it's easy to come to terms with the disappearance of your dream. Your dream is like the star of Bethlehem; it is always moving; appearing then disappearing until it finally stops at your destiny. In this respect, we follow the star but we find the Christ. If you follow your dreams what you will actually find is your destiny.

Again, the value is in the path and not in the dream because the path corrects and perfects; it refines and defines; it stretches and moulds your character into the person who fits the big picture called destiny. In this respect, the value is in what you are becoming as a result of your journey. Immature dream-chasers focus on what they are getting out of life. But the children of destiny value what they are becoming in life as a result of getting and giving; winning and losing, mountains and valleys.

Think of Joseph whose dream initiated a journey. After telling his brothers, they simply pushed him onto a path. The path would break him and remake him to manifest his destiny as the prince of Egypt. In his case, the value was not in the dream but in the path or process that would make him a prince. When Joseph's brothers finally met up with him, they didn't meet a bitter man, instead they met a better man. The reason why Joseph was not bitter, in his own words was this:

> ***And Joseph said unto his brethren, I am Joseph; doth my father yet live? And his brethren could not answer him; for they were troubled at his presence. 4] And Joseph said unto his brethren, Come near to me, I pray you. And they came near. And he said, I am Joseph your brother, whom ye sold into Egypt. 5] Now therefore be not grieved, nor angry with yourselves, that ye sold me hither: for God did send me before you to preserve life.***

> ***6] For these two years hath the famine been in the land: and yet there are five years, in the which there shall neither be earing nor harvest. 7] And God sent me before you to preserve you a posterity in the earth, and to save your lives by a great deliverance.***
>
> *Genesis 45:3-7*

Joseph realized that God himself had ordered his steps and that his path, though painful at times, was necessary for the manifestation of his destiny. When you look back over your life, do you see God ordering your steps or do you see a series of failures and disasters? As I look back over my life; I am not bitter at all. In fact I am much, much better and eternally grateful for the path that produced a prince in me.

I am grateful for the legalism, because it was like a boot camp that taught me the disciplines of self-control, sacrifice and obedience to authority. I am grateful for the years I espoused the evacuation theory because that's where I lost my attachment to worldly things. I am grateful for the domestic difficulties I experienced because they made me a realist. I am grateful to the people who left and those who stayed because they gave me the ultimate education in human nature. I am grateful for the debt, depression and divorce that I passed through on the pathway of purpose, because they birthed in me a deep compassion for humanity and new focus on the quality of life.

When you value the journey more than the dream; your destiny will appear.

CHAPTER 11

CIRCLES OF INFLUENCE

When I discovered the Kingdom, my understanding of the great commission changed. Up until that point I thought that evangelizing the world was the only authentic work of the church. Everything else was simply a means to that end. My understanding of the world was also limited to geography. Basically, we had to reach India, Africa, china, Europe and the Americas with the message of the cross. Only when this was done, could we expect the return of Christ.

Personal evangelism, mass evangelism and media campaigns were all part of our work. We had to spread the net over a geographic territory in order to catch men for Christ. However, the first thing that changed was my understanding of the world. The world is not simply made up of geo-political territories; it is also composed of social and economic systems, institutions and cultures. The Greek word that is used for the 'world' is the word 'kosmos'. The word forms the root of our English 'cosmetics'. It ultimately describes the world as an arrangement or organization of different components.

Go into all the world, could better read; go into every man's world. You really cannot go into all the world unless you go into the institutions, systems, cultures and sub-cultures that make up a society. It is simply not possible to reach the world unless you identify the components that make it up and then get inside them. The idea of going into the world was foreign to me because I had preached for so long that we should come out and be separate. I didn't realize that coming out of the world means spiritual insulation and was never intended to be an excuse for isolation.

> ***'Behold I send you forth as sheep in the midst of wolves...'***
>
> *Matthew 10:16*

The great commission was always meant to be an inside job. In other words you cannot stay on your side of the fence and shout over to the other side. You must first go in before you can get the message out. The problem with most evangelistic campaigns is that they attempt to preach the gospel from the outside. The Biblical formula is always to preach it from the inside. We were meant to go in first and only then to proclaim the good news throughout.

Having discovered this principle, of course I needed the patterns to authenticate it. As explained in previous chapters, the patterns were numerous for what I call; 'covert Kingdom operations'. I noticed that God specialized in planting his agents inside the very palaces of the kingdoms of men awaiting instructions for advancing the kingdom. They were like sleepers awaiting their orders from the HQ. This was true of Joseph,

Esther, Nehemiah and Daniel who each served God in the kingdoms of men awaiting instructions for advancing the Kingdom on earth.

THE WORLD

The world is a complex system of institutions, organisations, cultures and subcultures. In the Bible, they are called 'Kingdoms'. A kingdom is not just a geo-political territory. It is a king's domain. As such it constitutes any enterprise that is governed by a leader. In this respect; corporations, musical subcultures, public institutions and government itself is a Biblical kingdom. In this respect, any geographic territory may house hundreds or thousands of kingdoms. Take London, for example; it is a melting pot of cultures, class, subcultures, commerce, arts, media, historic institutions and religion. If London were simply a geo-political territory, then the gospel has already been preached here. Ask the man standing on a box in Hyde Park and he will say, 'Yes I preached the gospel in London'.

The only problem is that 10 million people never heard him. The great commission assumes an invasion. The first part of it says; 'Go ye into all the world...' Mark 16:15. This means that true evangelism is meant to be an inside job. It is supposed to be preached from inside out and not from the outside in. You first go in and then you preach.

PREACHING

The second thing that changed when I discovered the Kingdom was my understanding of what preaching really is. Up until that point I assumed that preaching meant telling, announcing or declaring. It was totally audible. However, the Word of God is both audible and visible. It is an audio/visual word. Jesus Christ himself is the Word of God who didn't just proclaim the gospel of the Kingdom but He also demonstrated the power and nature of that Kingdom. He preached with visual aids. These typically took the form of miracles and each miracle was designed to drive home a point.

The Apostle Paul said:

> ***1 And I, brethren, when I came to you,***
> ***came not with excellency of speech***
> ***or of wisdom, declaring unto you the***
> ***testimony of God. 2] For I determined***
> ***not to know any thing among you, save***
> ***Jesus Christ, and him crucified. 3] And I was***
> ***with you in weakness, and in fear, and in much***
> ***trembling. 4] And my speech and my preach-***
> ***ing was not with enticing words of man's***
> ***wisdom, but in demonstration of the Spirit***
> ***and of power: 5] That your faith should***
> ***not stand in the wisdom of men,***
> ***but in the power of God.***
>
> *1 Corinthians 2:1-5*

An audible presentation is often incomplete. Especially in the western world where humanistic philosophy is prevalent. Arguing about Jesus is not really evangelism. You have to take away the argument in order to make any ground. For example, pharaoh couldn't really argue with Joseph about God. Joseph was simply too valuable to him.

Joseph actually saved the kingdom of Egypt from utter ruin and his consulting and management services caused the Pharaoh to prosper during Egypt's greatest recession.

The same is true of Daniel who was so beloved by King Darius, that the king came to the mouth of the lions' den hoping against hope that Daniel's God had saved him from the lions.

I think you see where I might be going with this. If you add value to people, they will listen to you without an argument. It is difficult to argue with Love. How can you fight love? What debate do you hold with love? Nobody cares how much you know until they know how much you care. Lots of churches have now embraced the idea that the gospel should be preached in word and deed. Specifically acts of kindness, service and support. They are out in the community cleaning up, shopping for the elderly, providing activities for the youth, feeding the poor and housing the homeless. They are campaigning against crime and supporting its victims. Setting up shelters, soup kitchens and food banks. They are building relationships with drug addicts, prostitutes and gang members and are doing it all without a sermon, a lecture or a speech. Simply showing the unconditional love of Christ to fractured communities, has changed the status of many churches from being a social liability to becoming a social asset.

A STEP FURTHER

This idea of the church becoming a social asset is catching on. It means adding value to your community by giving something to it as opposed to taking things away from it. However, many are still struggling with the next logical step. We understand community engagement and are fast becoming the most valuable social asset in every community. However, community is only one circle or sphere of influence in a society and unfortunately it ranks at the very bottom of the list.

There are at least six other spheres or circles of influence that make up a society. The church as a whole is yet to view each of these as a mission field and is yet to mount a strategic invasion of these realms. Here they are:

(ONE) POLITICS

(ONE) POLITICS

Politics is the process by which individuals and groups determine the laws and policies that govern our society. Fortunately, we live in a democracy in which everyone is free to participate. There are numerous ways of participating both from within and without the parties and institutions that are overtly political. You can participate on a local level with your local authority by voting at bi-elections, by becoming a Counsillor or by campaigning for change. It is each citizen's right and role to elect representatives and then to hold them to account. After all, these representatives will tax you and then spend your money to realise their manifesto promises. Many believers sit by while this happens because they do not understand the system and because they don't have a Biblical framework for operating in this field. You can make this your mission field and go into this aspect of your world in many ways. The key is in locating your own passion. If you feel passionately about the impact that public policy has on the people you care for, then it may be that God is calling you into this field to become an irreplaceable asset to your party, your community or your country.

(TWO) BUSINESS

(TWO) BUSINESS

I have perhaps been criticised the most for my emphasis on self employment, entrepreneurship and business ownership. They said I was preaching the prosperity gospel of greed. To the contrary, I realised that the job market was shrinking and that public services would become thin. I knew that self-employment was the only realistic answer to growing unemployment and therefore provided enterprise training and selfemployment skills training to whoever would listen. As it turns out, I am now in demand for this very thing. However, it goes beyond the micro-economics of an income stream.

Business owners have powerful voices in society or at least have the money to make their voices heard. The church has been the beggar in society for long enough. It is now critical that more believers become CEO's and individuals of considerable substance through enterprise. This will give the gospel a sound economic base, without which most of our efforts will end in frustration. At the moment, large churches have become our economic base, however, this should change such that the economic base of the church is the enterprises which have come out of her. Because I am particularly passionate about this issue, I am in danger of writing too much. Let's just say; watch this space for more about economic bases and institutions that could come out of the church including banks, venture capital and large corporations.

(THREE) MEDIA

(THREE) MEDIA

The media is powerful beyond description. It literally creates our perception of reality. How do you know what is going on in the world? The media tells you! As such it is a force for good and evil. Good if it holds power to account and evil if it is manipulated by power to create false impressions. The media can make or break any individual and for that reason, it is a circle of influence that should not be ignored by kingdom minded believers. Whether main stream or independent, the media is a kingdom waiting for a Joseph, Esther, Nehemiah or a Daniel to serve it adding immense value and generating favour. Again, the idea is influence. If you can rise to the top of your field or become an adviser to those at the top, you may be able to use that influence in a way that puts the church in a positive light. The church is often vilified by the media who do not want to be seen Rooting any faith besides humanism. This is partly because our society at large is that way but also because there are too few believers occupying its higher ranks.

(FOUR) EDUCATION

(FOUR) EDUCATION

I learned this lesson during an argument with a teacher who asked me not to refer to my boy as a champion. He felt that this term gave him false hope and that a more realistic approach to parenting would be to prepare him for life as a basic wage employee. I gave him a brief lesson in psychology and then moved my boy from the school. Teachers are all too often stressed by a Job that has become less about teaching and more about passing government inspections. No one seriously disputes the fact that our education system is broken. It fails many a genius whose primary intelligence doesn't fit the teaching methods employed by the school. My view, as expressed in my book, 'The Mis-Education of the masses', is that it is broken on the strategic level. Its strategy is still linked to the illusion of job security and does little to nurture entrepreneurship. Further more, many of the staff are over worked and under paid, the result being that many children in deprived areas do not get the start that they deserve. Surely this is a mission field for those who understand the true nature of the gospel.

(FIVE) ENTERTAINMENT

Entertainers are the prophets of the new age. With fan bases in the millions they typically have more influence on social norms than do preachers and politicians. Check your YouTube views. See if you can find a preacher with more views than the top pop, hip-hop and R&B artists? What about film stars? Do you notice them getting more involved in politics and elections? The reason that they are of value to politicians is that they have a captive audience of millions through Twitter, Facebook and YouTube. Entertainment is still a difficult field for many Christians however, kingdom minded, amphibious and bilingual believers who are insulated and unintimidated by the culture of entertainment, can go in and rise to the top. This is a major mission field and mountain that needs to be conquered if the great commission is going to be fulfilled.

(FIVE) ENTERTAINMENT

(SIX) RELIGION

(SIX) RELIGION

I was recently on a mission trip to Indonesia where I sponsored a child through Compassion UK. Together with a group of preachers we surveyed the work of local churches in a predominantly Muslim country. Something happened on that trip that sparked controversy and a heated conversation for the rest of the journey. We visited an area that had been devastated by an earthquake. The people had lost their homes and belongings and were now living in tents and fabricated accommodation. Much of that accommodation was built by local churches in partnership with relief charities and agencies. The shock was that, in addition to providing accommodation, the church also built a make shift Mosque for the community of predominant Muslims. Many of the preachers didn't get it. How can the church build a Mosque? Why would the church build a Mosque? However, a few us did get it. We realised that through this single act of kindness, the church had successfully shattered all perceptions of Christianity as a bigoted, elitist and anti-Muslim religion. Instead the church became a social asset. By recognising the need for a battered community to feel close to God and knowing that it could only do so in a Mosque, the church demonstrated true compassion and a certain superiority of conscience.

Something happened on that trip that sparked controversy and a heated conversation for the rest of the journey.

When the fanatical Muslims later attempted to burn down the local church, it was the Muslim community that rose up against them and vowed to protect the church with their very life. I know that this story doesn't sit well with religious Christians but it certainly sits well with kingdom people. Religion is a massive circle of influence and it takes a special grace to become a source of cohesion, collaboration and better understanding between people of differing faiths.

I HAVE A DREAM

I have been chasing dreams all my life only to discover that they were only ever a glimpse of destiny. They provided light in the tunnels of time and set my life on the pathways of purpose.

I now have a dream that the circles of power and influence in societies across the world, will harbour kingdom people like Joseph, Esther, Nehemiah and Daniel. Modern day missionaries who enter the social and economic mission fields of power, bringing value and service to the people of the world. I dream of politicians who love Jesus, billionaires who pray in the Spirit; Oxford and Cambridge professors who operate in the spiritual gifts, actors, actresses, singers and musicians like Bono who, although adored by millions of secular fans, can still sing praises to God on stage. I dream that the scientist who discovers a cure for aids and cancer will glorify God for giving him or her the breakthrough.

I dream of a ministry whose main aim is to equip believers for a life of service in the circles of power. The poverty of aspiration and the lack of ambition is a curse that confines the church to the realms of insignificance. I dream of an aspirational awakening until, like Caleb and Joshua, a generation will set their sights on the real promised Land.

Can you imagine what would happen if our young people had audacious and ambitious goals to change the world? It's bold, it's audacious, it's crazy but it's what I have become through the process of transformation. What is even more crazy is that I fully intend to implement a strategy to see it come to pass.

Pray for me!

CHAPTER 12

LESSONS FROM MY LIFE

Life comes loaded with lessons and packed with principles designed to guide and steer you along the pathway of purpose. As I look back over mine, there are some important lessons that I use as leverage for a better future. The same can be said of your life. It is as though God is teaching you today what you will need to know tomorrow. You may not learn much from my lessons but hopefully you will be inspired and motivated to look back over your own life, gleaning both the power for the present and fuel for the future.

Here are mine:

KNOW THAT YOU ARE UNCONDITIONALLY AND COMPLETELY LOVED BY GOD.

Human love is limited by knowledge. They only love what they know about you. Subconsciously we all know this and that is why we only tell our deepest secrets to our closest friends. The more people know the less they may love. However, God knows all there is to know about you; past, present and future. His love is real, it's unconditional and it is everlasting.

UNDERSTAND THAT SALVATION IS A GIFT TO BE RECEIVED AND NOT A REWARD TO BE EARNED.

There is nothing a man can do to merit eternal life. Your hope must be built on nothing less than Jesus' blood and his righteousness. Sin will not keep you out of heaven but it will hinder your progress on planet earth. Sin is disobedience to an instruction that God gives you. Not the instructions He gave to an ancient people whose culture and circumstance have since perished. You should attempt to lose your sin-consciousness because whatever you focus on manifests itself in your life. Instead you should focus on God's love and his purposes. This is difficult for the legalistic mind because it sounds like I am opening the cage. Please remember that you cannot tame the lion in a cage, you can only tame it once it gets out. The Holy Spirit and the Scriptures will guide you in matters pertaining to lifestyle but do not make this your magnificent obsession as though your eternity depended on it.

KNOW THAT YOU WERE BORN TO WIN AND BORN TO FLY

A caterpillar is a baby butterfly. It cannot fly at birth but after its transformation in a dark and solitary place it develops wings and flys. You were born to win but your true beauty may not appear until you have been moulded by adversity.

IT DOESN'T MATTER WHERE YOU START; WHAT MATTERS IS HOW YOU FINISH

Whatever disadvantages you inherited at birth cannot prevent you from becoming the butterfly that you are. The past does not equal the future. Instead, your past contains the lessons and fuel for a better and brighter future. Draw out the lessons and convert the pain into fuel.

KNOW THAT YOUR DESTINY IS BIGGER THAN YOUR DREAMS

Your dreams are the small picture that you see but your destiny is the big picture that only God sees. It is the Divine purpose for which you were born at this time and in that place. Only God knows how many millions of lives will be impacted by yours. However, you must follow your dreams because they will lead you to your destiny.

DECIDE TO FOLLOW YOUR DREAMS BECAUSE THEY WILL LEAD TO YOUR DESTINY

Following your dreams requires true courage because the journey is deliberately designed to change you. The journey teaches you everything needed to manifest your destiny. In this respect your life is your main teacher. In the cocoon, a caterpillar literally digests itself until its own organs become fluid. This then allows them to reset in the form and shape of a butterfly. Digesting yourself means converting the lessons of your past into fuel for the future.

DECIDE TO INVADE A CIRCLE OF INFLUENCE

Your destiny is what you were born to be. But being is the key to doing. You are here to do something for the progress of humanity and to protect heaven's interests on earth. Stop obsessing about a role in your church and instead begin looking for a role in society. There are seven circles or spheres of influence in society as follows: Politics, business, media, entertainment, education, religion and family/community. If religion is your sphere then by all means serve your church and develop your spiritual senses but if not then don't feel that a role in government or in business or in the community is somehow inferior.

DECIDE TO GROW

There is a difference between talent and skill. Talent is a natural or genetic advantage. But skill is developed through hours of discipline. Don't rely on talent alone to get you through life. Instead you should turn your talent into a skill through diligence and discipline. Decide to expand your vocabulary, particularly in the circle to which you are called. Make learning a priority by building a library of books, audios, articles, publications and blogs. Feed on the Scriptures in a daily devotion and learn how to pray. Build your capacity to achieve any goal that you set for yourself. Finally, you should strive for the mastery. This means committing to excellence and becoming the best that you can be.

CONVERT THE PAIN OF THE PAST INTO FUEL FOR THE FUTURE

Pain is a motivator in that it demands an immediate response. The good news is that you can choose your response. Allow the pain of your past to fuel your future. Simply decide that success is the sweetest revenge and the only true compensation for your struggles. Define your own success and do not allow others to define it for you. Then determine to achieve it using the pain of the past as your fuel.

KNOW THAT TRANSFORMATION OCCURS IN DARKNESS AND NOT IN LIGHT

When ever you find yourself in a dark place, know that it is for the purpose of transformation and that transformation is a prelude to manifestation. The cocoon will change your shape and enhance your capacity to achieve success. It is a necessary part of the journey that is designed to change you into the person who fits the future. The darkness holds secrets and lessons will be learned in that season which you could not get from a text book. Cherish them and use them for the future.

KNOW THAT TRANSFORMATION PRECEDES MANIFESTATION

If you are right now experiencing transformation in the dark cocoon of a fiery trial, then know that you are on the brink of a breakthrough and the verge of victory. Transformation happens in darkness but manifestation happens in light. Weeping may endure for a night but joy cometh in the morning. Divine days are made up of an evening and a morning. This means that a new day in God starts in the evening. The Jews define evening as sunset. In this respect a new day starts in the darkness but bursts into the light. Know that a new day has begun for you.

MAKE THE TRANSITION FROM CHURCH TO THE KINGDOM

A churchy Christian is concerned only with religion. A kingdom Christian is concerned with advancing and protecting heaven's interests on earth. A churchy Christian is waiting and hoping for an imminent evacuation from this sinful world while a kingdom Christian is attempting to invade its institutions and systems. A churchy Christian practises isolation and remains disconnected from the community in which they congregate, but a kingdom Christian practises insulation, with amazing grace for their space, they remain connected to communities and society at large.

KNOW THAT YOUR STRENGTHS AND WEAKNESSES ARE USED BY GOD TO MANIFEST YOUR DESTINY

Whether they be physical, psychological or spiritual, your weaknesses serve a specific purpose in the plan of God for your life. Without them you cannot discover grace and would never know the true power of God. You would also fail to understand or identify with the human condition. The fact is that we are all fundamentally flawed and literally incapable of perfect obedience. Your weaknesses should birth compassion in you for others who struggle too. God uses your weaknesses and your strengths to pull you along the path that would eventually manifest your destiny. Don't despise your weaknesses. Instead know that God's grace is sufficient for you.

KNOW THAT CIRCUMSTANCES DO NOT DEFINE YOU, THEY REFINE YOU

Part of my depression came from allowing my circumstances to define me. I was a failure because my marriage had failed, my ministry had failed and my finances had failed. However when grace appeared to me I realised that failure is an event and not a person. I also learned that failure is a code word for feedback. Life was giving me feedback about what was important and what was not. What worked and what didn't. When I allowed the circumstances to refine me, I came out of it a better person. I had changed; the same Wayne but now I had a pair of wings.

KNOW THAT WHERE YOU ARE DOESN'T TELL US WHO YOU ARE

The path that will manifest your destiny will take you through highs and lows. Good people in the Bible often found themselves in prison, in a wilderness, in a furnace or a den, even on an old rugged cross. But where you are doesn't tell us who you are. You simply could not know that Joseph was destined to be the prince of Egypt if you met him in the slave market, on sale to Potiphar. Likewise no one has the right to write you off based on your current circumstances. God will use them to make you and manifest your ultimate destiny.

NEVER CONFUSE YOUR IDENTITY WITH YOUR ADDRESS

You are not your circumstances. You are not your weight, your shape, your colour or your career. You possess these but they are not you. You are fundamentally spiritual in nature and as a spirit being, you have intrinsic value beyond any treasure on planet earth. Don't ever lose sight of your immense worth to God and to others. Do not confuse yourself with the things you do or have. Never link your worth to your work. You are worth much more than these. The ultimate proof of your worth is the cross. Why would Christ pay the ultimate price for you if you were a worthless failure. Clearly He knows something about us that we do not know about ourselves.

REINVENT YOUR SELF OFTEN

The caterpillar moults and sheds its skin several times before its final metamorphosis into a butterfly. I never understood this but a careful reading of my story will show that I changed several times before reaching the conclusions that would come to define my life. Now I love change. I'm neither addicted to my ideas nor my initiatives. Instead I am constantly learning, evolving and becoming a better me. The path of the just is as a shining light that shines more and more until the perfect day.

STAY TRUE TO THE LIGHT

As you grow, your understanding will change. You will see things differently or at least more clearly. The light is the still, small voice of conviction. It is ultimately your faith! Staying true to it means allowing it to take you on an adventure but never holding it to an outcome. That adventure is designed to change you into a glorious butterfly but it will come at a cost. Some people are proud of the fact that they have never changed their position. They get celebrated for believing the same things they always believed. However for me this is a mark of extreme immaturity and the proof that that person stopped growing.

CONCLUSION

I wrote this book because I sense that I am not alone. There are perhaps millions of others who are likewise on the pathways of purpose; following their convictions yet confused by a chain of events that are seemingly beyond their control. Like Joseph, many have chased a dream only to find themselves in an emotional prison, shrouded by allegation and uncertain about the future. The fact that convictions cost and that they initially produce loss is not always clear to those convicted of a truth.

When I came to Christ, I lost an entire circle of worldly friends who did not understand my new conviction and with that, I lost my status as leader of the pack. But I gained Christ and an amazing life filled with adventure. When I embraced grace, I likewise lost an entire circle of friends, colleagues, opportunities and statuses that were stooped in religion and legalistic ideology. Some felt I had left the faith, backslidden and lost the plot. Others privately expressed support but could not come out in the open for fear of reprisals. In fact; I have lost entire circles of friendships, status and opportunity on at least 4 separate occasions and all in the name of a conviction.

This of course calls into question the nature of those friendships. All over the world I continue to meet people who hunger for authentic relationships as opposed to the ones fabricated in organisations, denominations and companies. The problem is that you can only have an authentic relationship with an authentic person and personal authenticity is difficult to discover, let alone display in an environment where your livelihood depends on the fabrication. In other words, in an environment where authenticity (doing you) may cost you everything, the culture of that environment will fabricate false relationships with false people. If everyone is wearing a mask, how do you connect with anyone? If taking off the mask will cost you everything then should you really take it off?

These questions among many sit in the psyche of an emerging new breed who are disillusioned with business as usual. I know many ministers who would jump out of their denominations and out of their churches today if they could. Unfortunately their livelihoods are linked to the system and the cost of following a conviction seems too great to bare. For all the talk of church growth; recent statistics show that the rate at which ministers are leaving the ministry is at an all time high. These are the ones that have a second trade and can quit without losing their life. As a vocation; the ministry feels unsafe and uncertain for many ministers who are afraid to be human. The mantra for many ministers is the same; I want real and genuine relationships. They join networks, fellowships and associations in search of an authentic circle of friends with whom they can be human without the fear of criticism, reprisal or worse yet; gossip.

A fabricated culture of false relationships only serves to suppress problems that could have been resolved if people were allowed to be real. These cultures breed secrecy and the secrecy gives power to the issues at hand.

Real friends make a real difference because they allow for the formation of the butterfly. If anyone interferes with the butterfly in the cocoon they will kill it. The key is to allow the struggle whilst loving that which is being formed. A few friends were that way for me. They loved me; warts and all, title or no title, big ministry or small, broke or rich! They saw the struggle and simply loved me through it because they knew that something precious would come out of it. Others wanted to dive in and fix or correct or refine what was really the making of a new me. With all their great intentions they would have only served to kill what was really in formation.

Needless to say, I do not miss any fabricated friendships, neither do I miss the status that comes with wearing the best mask. There are friends in my life today who couldn't care less about my position, titles, performance or circumstances. They are connected to me as though destiny demanded it and I to them. We have no business relationship, we are not profiting from one another and definitely don't agree on everything. Instead our authenticity is the commonality that attracts us to each other. The fact that we are free souls who can think out of the box, express an opinion and be completely honest without fear makes us an amazing match.

The Bible says:

> ***But the path of the just is as the shining light, that shineth more and more unto the perfect day.***
>
> *Proverbs 4:18*

As I understand it; a just path comes with a progressive light. There is less light at the beginning and more light as you go. You are supposed to see more light as you go. Your understanding should evolve and with it your capacity to manifest your destiny.

The courage to follow your convictions is becoming a rare commodity in today's world where acceptance, affirmation and celebration are coveted more than the pursuit of purpose. However there are many millions of ambitious souls who are on the true path of the just. They are following a progressive light like the wise men who followed the star of Bethlehem. They are disillusioned by doctrines of men that disempower the soul and instead, seek a more authentic expression of the faith that liberates rather than limits their true potential.

I wrote this book to connect with and to encourage the emerging breed of believers whom I believe will genuinely fulfil the great commission of Christ. The authentic, amphibious and bilingual ambassadors of the kingdom. Among them are those who want to take their music mainstream; they are in the arts and entertainment industries; business and politics, media and community programmes.They are in the system or trying to get into it but can not bring the obnoxious religiosity of traditional Christianity in with them. I meet them all the time; confused about how far they can go in entertainment, in politics or in business. Wondering if they should be less ambitious and more pious. It is as though their faith and their life are at war and they feel as though one will eventually kill the other.

I want to connect with those who are in the process of transformation; dealing with the loss of some things and struggling to free themselves from a cocoon. I want to tell them that grace is sufficient and that what they are becoming in life is more important than what they are getting out of it.

The mystical truth and secret of the butterfly is that the process is the prize. The value was always in the path because it is the path that breaks, makes, moulds and reshapes you for destiny. New things definitely won't make a new you, but a new you will definitely attract new things. Wherever you are right now in life is part of a perfect plan to transform the caterpillar into a butterfly. A caterpillar is, in fact, a baby butterfly! May you manifest your destiny and glorify God with your amazing life.

Warts an' all lol.

ALSO BY BISHOP WAYNE MALCOLM IN THIS SERIES

BUTTERFLY STRATEGIES (WORKBOOK)

Another excellent resource that goes hand in hand with *'The Butterfly Secret'* is *'Butterfly Strategies'.* (Work-book) This study aid has 21 Biblical strategies for personal transformation.

THE BUTTERFLY SECRET (ABRIDGED AUDIO BOOK)

Hear the author, Bishop Wayne Malcolm read through carefully selected extracts from *'The Butterfly Secret'.*
This excellent resource will help you go over the more challenging aspects of this book again and again.

THESE AND OTHER RESOURCES CAN BE FOUND AT

www.icanministries.co.uk